To: ▪▪▪▪▪▪▪▪▪▪▪▪▪▪▪▪▪▪▪▪▪▪▪▪

Thomas L. Pyatt

An artistic preservation of the history of a unique people and their culture, through art, writings, books, etc. As seen from the perspective and vantage point of a Gullah native son.

GULLAH HISTORY
ALONG THE CAROLINA
LOWCOUNTRY

ISBN 0-9767079-3-4

ISBN 0-9767079-3-4

Many generations have come and gone, but they all kept a yearning, a burning desire to return to their roots as much as possible over the years. Many of the younger generation was away working and living in other areas, but they always returned to the area to be with their elders and renew their roots deep down within them. The legacy was within them and will always be with them and all of us.

May God continue to bless you throughout the coming years.

Thomas J. Pyatt

Dedication

This book is dedicated to the legacy of the independent and hard working Gullah people who have struggled for decades to make life better for each succeeding generation. They have kept alive the traditions of their ancestors in the midst of insurmountable odds, and have retained their unique Gullah culture throughout the centuries to this present day. Their struggles and commitment to excellence and self sufficiency have made it better for all who have followed in their footsteps.

Time has changed many communities as there are now some major developments in the traditional Gullah communities. And even though many communities and historic sites have been lost due to such major developments and changes, the people continue on. Many historic sites and old freedmen's villages and some old graveyards have been built over and are now gone; but they will live on in our memories and documentation of such a glorious past.

I had the opportunity to observe such fortitude by the Gullah people, as I was born and raised in a Gullah community in a riverfront town by the Waccamaw River deep down in the southeast. This book is another step in the artistic preservation of the history of a unique people and their culture. A documentation of experiences and efforts to make life and living better for all who came in contact with them over the decades and generations. You have truly taught us the meaning of taking a journey deep down back home. It is truly wonderful to take such a journey back to our roots.

Contents

Introduction

The Carolina Lowcountry has been home to the Gullah People for centuries. The Lowcountry consists of the coastal areas and Sea Islands, and the Lowcountry is known for its good fertile grounds. The Gullah People are descendants of the residents of West Africa who were involuntarily brought to these shores centuries ago to work the fertile coastal areas as slaves. They came through the ports of Angola and the Congo, from Goree Island, Senegal and Bunce Island, Sierra Leone, etc. The Gullah-Geechee culture is alive and well in the Carolinas, Florida and Georgia. The people are all descendants of the residents of West Africa who were involuntarily brought to these shores centuries ago. They are known as Geechee in Georgia and Florida, and as Gullah in the Carolinas; from about Jacksonville, N.C. to about Jacksonville, Florida. Some of the communities have changed, some are changing and some are gone.

I was born and raised in South Carolina along the coast about 14 miles from the Atlantic Ocean, in the Old Historic Riverfront Town of Conway. My father was born and raised on Sandy Island, S.C., an isolated island that is still the home to some Gullah people. The state of South Carolina now owns a little over 75% of Sandy Island, and the Gullah settlements or communities are still located on the eastern quarter of the island. Many of the Gullah people there still reside on land passed down to them from the prior generations. I often visited Sandy Island when I was young and spent many summers on the island as a young child growing up. I had some great experience and have many memories of the Gullah people there, as well as many of the surrounding areas all up and down the coast of the Carolina Lowcountry.

I will concentrate on the Gullah people and their communities or settlements because I am Gullah, and I have seen many of the communities changed, changing or gone, as a result of major developments, especially over the last decade or so. The Gullah communities were more defined or pronounced after post reconstruction than they are today. The Gullah settlements today are, and can be referred to as Gullah communities; we referred to them as settlements in the 1950's when I was growing up in the area. Many of us subsequently migrated away to jobs and careers and resided elsewhere for decades. Now that many of us have retired after over 40 years in the workforce; many of us have returned to our Gullah roots in retirement, to help preserve our rich culture and heritage.

Many of our parents (that generation) resided in the Carolina Lowcountry in or close to their childhood homes and hometowns all of their lives. Many of them here in the county where I grew up remained close to the Waccamaw River, which for centuries has supported an abundance of life. Opportunities for them did not exist as it did for my generation and beyond, therefore they remained close to their land just as their forefathers before them. Their sacrifices made it easier for me to travel and get a good education in an effort to make life and living better for all. Their sacrifices will always be greatly appreciated, as we continue on.

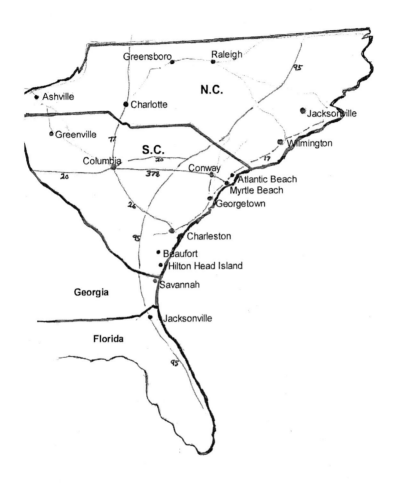

Gullah Communities
The Customs, Habits and Folkways of a People

The Gullah-Geechee people have a very rich history and culture that has remained virtually intact for centuries in their new land. They are descendants of the West Africans who were involuntarily brought here to work as slaves on the plantations and fertile grounds of the Carolina Lowcountry; and they have retained their heritage, history and culture throughout the centuries. It has been estimated that over a third of the Blacks in America today can trace their history through the ports of Charleston, S.C. or nearby "Pest Houses" etc. This was the height of the slave trade between 1700 and 1800. During the middle passage they came from Ghana, the ports of Angola and the Congo, Buncee Island on Sierra Leone and Goree Island on Senegal. The indigenous West African Cultural traditions survived, and are still flourishing today.

The customs, habits and folkways of the people of West Africa is alive today in the Carolina Lowcountry and Sea Islands. The good traditions have been passed down from generation to generation throughout the centuries. Tourists are flocking to the Carolina Lowcountry to visit the many plantations, etc. that offer guided tours of their historic sites. There is a wealth of history here all up and down the Carolina Lowcountry and various Sea Islands. There are various museums and events at the Penn Center on St. Helena Island during the year. In Charleston there are other archives, Old Slave Mart, etc.

As I grew up in my Gullah community along the Waccamaw River in our old historic Riverfront Town, it was more of a rural settlement or small community back in the 1950's. As we grew up in our little isolated communities we were very aware of our rich culture and heritage. Our parents and community instilled in us a sense of self worth and taught us the knowledge of self, and our history. The pillars of the community were the family, church and school, and we had some extremely dedicated teachers in our Gullah schools. We learned the value of work at a young age, as we could see that our parents and ancestors worked hard for the little that they had. They did not have and could not afford a lot of material things in life, but they were content and lived a peaceful and productive life. They succeeded with a lot less than we have today. At a young age I noticed their independence and ingenuity and will to succeed among and against all odds. It was instilled in me at a very young age that I too could succeed with study and hard work, and be able to give back to my community.

The opportunities were severely limited in the 1950's and I knew that if I kept studying hard and migrated away to study and work, that I too would one day return to document this unique lifestyle along the Carolina Lowcountry and Sea Islands.

I was aware of many of the other Gullah communities as I was growing up, but I didn't have the means to visit all of the other areas all up and down the Carolina Lowcountry. Our High School team (The Old Whittemore High School) played football, basketball and baseball games against many of the high school teams in the other Gullah communities in the surrounding areas. The old school bus back in those days would only go 35 miles an hour, so it would sometimes take quite a while to go a little ways. The limited competition was very rewarding for all of us, and a chance to meet people from other communities.

We also took other trips on the old slow school buses besides just going to athletic events. I remember going to picnics and field trips to Atlantic Beach, as it was the only beach open to us in the 1950's. I also knew about some of the old plantations, as we had to go through Brookgreen Gardens to get to the old Sandy Island Landing, to go across the Waccamaw River to get to the old boat dock on Sandy Island. The Waccamaw River was and still is a mighty and ferocious black water river, and is one of the few black water rivers in the world. It always looked muddy to me and nothing like the water at the beach, and I therefore always respected that mighty river, especially when I had to cross it in a small rowboat. Sandy Island is in Georgetown County and the Waccamaw River ran all the way past my hometown in Horry County.

I grew up in the county seat of Conway in Horry County, and it is still that old historic Riverfront Town by the Waccamaw River. Our Gullah high school in Conway was the old Whittemore High School, and Gullah children came from all over the county to go to high school at Whittemore, as it was the only high school that they could attend in the county in the 1950's. Many of my friends and cousins came from Myrtle Beach and the surrounding towns to go to the old Whittemore High School. The Whittemore community was a main and central community back in those days. I had some early knowledge of the Gullah communities all up and down the Carolina Lowcountry, even though I couldn't afford to visit all the areas at that time. Just being classmates with all the other students from all the surrounding towns and pocket communities gave me a closer connection to those communities. Some of them are still residing in the area, and have been there since we graduated from high school all those decades ago.

6

I knew then that the history and culture of these communities should be documented and preserved. That the life and history of these brave and hard working people should be documented and preserved, and told to subsequent generations. I knew of and about some of the old plantations in the Carolina Lowcountry as the elders told us about them as they had worked on some of them as they were growing up.

I knew about the history of the Gullah people of Georgetown County, where my parents were from, and all the way to Charleston and beyond. We took an end of year school trip in the 1950's to Charleston to visit the museums, and they were full of colonial history, but no Gullah history. I had heard a little about the Penn Center in Beaufort County, but I didn't get a chance to visit it then. My father had told me about the history of Brookgreen Gardens, and the Atalya House at Huntington Beach across from Brookgreen Gardens. My father spent his childhood on Sandy Island growing up, and my mother grew up in Plantersville, across the Pee Dee River on the western border of Sandy Island. She told me about working on some of the plantations in the area, and how they would often walk from Plantersville to Georgetown, a distance of about 12 miles.

I knew that there were a lot of farming communities all over the area, as many of the students that commuted to the old Whittemore High School lived on farms in rural areas. The many small family farms were a way of life for the prior Gullah generation, and for us growing up in the 1950's. Farming was a major factor in helping a number of Gullah communities become independent during post reconstruction. Former slaves worked the land and eventually acquired some land to pass down to subsequent generations, in spite of various obstacles.

This was quite a feat considering that there were major obstacles in the sharecropping arrangements. Our ancestors had limited educational, economic, and no political opportunities, but they did have a very strong belief in God, and they accomplished much. They succeeded with a lot less than we have today, and they worked hard so that we may have a better life today. I remember telling my mother decades ago what I would like to do with my art and books when I get more opportunities. My mother told me exactly what to do, and how to prepare myself for what I wanted to do, and accomplish later in life as opportunities arose. Those words of wisdom were something that I will never forget, and they remain true even to this day. I wanted to be self sufficient and independent just like my parents and their generation, and I am grateful that I had the opportunity to observe their fortitude and determination.

The prior generation had a lot less formal education than we have, but they had an acute business sense and owned businesses in the community. They had an economic agenda that kept them off public assistance (as there was no welfare). They had a strong foundation which to build upon, even during the days of post reconstruction, the Gullah community was strong. I knew of this to some extent when I was growing up in the county during the 1950's and going to the old Whittemore High School there. I knew of the heroics of some of the Carolina Lowcountry's Blacks during and before post reconstruction. I knew that they manned ships during the civil war, even though they were not supposed to. I knew that the first Black in the United States House of Representatives was, Joseph Hayne Rainey from Georgetown, S.C. We studied to some extent about some Blacks and roles they played, and ship battles in the area during the civil war.

8

I knew that there were many more heroes from in and around the Sea Islands and along the Carolina Lowcountry. Over the decades much has changed along the Carolina Lowcountry, as major development has come and is continuing to come, especially to the areas closest to the Atlantic Ocean. This is also in the areas where many of the Gullah communities had strived for decades and generations. A half century or so ago it was thought to be only suitable for farming, and not too desirable. But today, the Myrtle Beach Grand Strand area with its many beaches is a major tourist attraction, and many people have migrated to the area and invested in the area.

What was once considered little backwoods small town country communities are not rural anymore, they have now become suburbs and the land is more valuable today. Many of the long time Gullah locals have been priced out of their long time communities because of the rising real estate costs due to major developments all over the areas. Their lives have changed and are a-changing in what were once their complete and total little hide-away communities.

The county is now fast becoming developed and even some golf courses have sold out to big developers because there is such a big demand for living near the ocean. Therefore, lifestyles have changed and some Gullah communities have changed, and some have been overtaken and lost by development. Even now when I drive by and through some of the old Gullah communities, I see memories of years past that will never come back, but such memories will never be lost because they are recorded within us forever. We have much to record and document and pass such memories and a special part of our heritage to future generations.

9

Changes have come to many of the old Gullah communities near the ocean such as, Atlantic Beach, the Hill on Myrtle Beach, McKenzie Beach (Magnolia Beach) and other little pocket communities such as, Murrells Inlet, Pawleys Island, Burgess, Socastee, Georgetown to Charleston and beyond. Beaufort County is now a Gullah focal point, and the Penn Center is located there. Many of the areas and communities near the ocean are being developed now that there is a tremendous demand for oceanfront condominiums. Major development and change is coming to Atlantic Beach, the only beach that we could go to during the 1950's.

Atlantic Beach – The Glory Years

Atlantic Beach is often referred to as The Black Pearl, as it was a Black beach resort for Blacks from the 1930's to the 1970's. Atlantic Beach was born out of segregation, and during that era the wealthy beachfront property owners that came to spend the summers wanted someplace for their servants to go to enjoy the ocean. When I was growing up in the county in the 1950's, Atlantic Beach was a wonderful Gullah community and the place to be on a hot summer day. It was only a few blocks long, but I have many fond memories of those days at the beach in the ocean on hot days with the mighty waves a-roaring cooling us off. The Atlantic Ocean was still enjoyable and refreshing on our little portion of the beach.

Atlantic Beach is now surrounded on three sides by North Myrtle Beach, and is bordered on the east by the Atlantic Ocean. Atlantic Beach was kind of quasi dormant for decades, and has come back to some extent, but not close to what it was during its glory years. Major developers have acquired some of the land closest to the ocean, and change is a-coming. It is now in the process of being developed by big developers, as there is still a big demand for the oceanfront condominiums.

Progress marches on even when small communities are lost, misplaced or realigned in the process. It is up to this current generation to record and preserve this critical part of our heritage and culture, so that future generations will have a first person account of what it was like in those glory years. Atlantic Beach was alive and bustling in it's heyday until the early 1970's. I remember going there in the 1950's and the 1960's.

It was nice and clean and peaceful back in those days and truly a family beach. We could use the porches of some of the beachfront houses as a place to change into our swimming trunks after we arrived at the beach on a school outing.

We often chose Atlantic Beach to come to on a school year end event. Many of the students from Whittemore High School came and enjoyed the 35 miles per hour ride from Conway, about 25 miles away. In the 1950's the school buses didn't go but 35 miles per hour, and that was by design by the state. But it didn't matter how long it took us to get there, as we just wanted to get there and enjoy the wonderful Atlantic Ocean and have a good outing. There were various restaurants around with outdoor patios where one could sit outdoors and enjoy the cool ocean breeze as they relaxed to eat.

After I graduated and moved away to California, I would often reflect on the down home times that I experienced at Atlantic Beach. It was one of the extra curricular activities that I missed most. On visits during my summer vacations it just seemed like the time went by so fast, and by the time I really got comfortable in reliving past good times at Atlantic Beach, it was time to return to California to go back to work. I was aware of the other beaches all up and down the Myrtle Beach Grand Strand area, but we could not visit them at that time.

Over the past few decades Atlantic Beach has attracted fewer visitors as the other beaches began opening up for us. Fewer visitors meant less tax dollars and curtailed services, and the area fell into neglect due to a lack of funds. The tourists went to the other beaches along the Grand Strand where development was expanding.

But now that there is such a big demand for more oceanfront condominiums, the land fronting the ocean on Atlantic Beach is in tremendous demand, and big developers are developing the area to fulfill the demands. There are plans for over 400 oceanfront condominiums to be built on the oceanfront at Atlantic Beach. It has taken a long time for major development to come to Atlantic Beach, but it is coming and the beach will never again be quite the same, but our memories and memoirs will keep the old spirit alive and well.

Atlantic Beach is surrounded on three sides by North Myrtle Beach and the Atlantic Ocean on the other side. Many changes have come, but I will always remember Atlantic Beach for what it was and the way it was during its glory years, and for the memories it gave me. But there is still the Hill Section of Myrtle Beach, and it too had a glorious past and is still going fairly strong even today.

The Glory Years were back when we roamed
the area and enjoyed the wonderful environment
and natural settings of our rural areas

We had some wonderful days all over the area
and I especially enjoyed playing baseball and
my wonderful experiences at the old
Whittemore High School

In the early days at our house we only had
kerosene lamps to light our house; but the great
light from above always shined brightly and led
the way for us to follow

The Hill on Myrtle Beach

A major section of the Black community on Myrtle Beach was and still is referred to as The Hill. The night life on The Hill was primarily on Carver Street, and it had most of the little motels, restaurants, night clubs, etc. in its glorious heyday. I remember it from the 1950's even though I was too young to go into the night clubs; I could hear the music a-playing. The Hill was also a magnet for some of the big name black musicians that stopped over on their way from the northeast on their way to Florida. Some big name stars stayed and played on The Hill in Myrtle Beach, and Charlie's Place was a main attraction and place to be, with lodging and a bar.

During the 1940's and 1950's when the Black tourists and musicians were traveling from the northeast to Florida on highway 17, they needed a place to stop over, and The Hill was the place. Such big name stars such as, Louis Jordan, Lena Horne, Duke Ellington, Billy Eckstein, Count Basie, Ray Charles, etc. were just a few that stopped over and played there on The Hill. Such big name stars also stayed and played at McKenzie Beach, a Black beach resort a little farther south on the Waccamaw Neck.

Carver Street is still a main street on The Hill in Myrtle Beach even today, but it has changed greatly now. The old motels are now closed and most have been demolished. A new generation is on the blocks in the neighborhoods now, and things have changed quite a bit. I often drive through the neighborhoods now just as I did over the decades when I came to visit the area and the old faces and places have faded away and moved on.

17

Some of my relatives, a new generation now reside in the neighborhoods and nearby. Carver Street is not as lively as it used to be in decades past, as the activities on the street has changed quite a bit. Major development has come closer to the area now and has almost surrounded the area. Broadway at the Beach is now not too far away, near the highway 17 bypass. A friend of mine has a business on Carver Street, and we were talking one day and he said we are now sitting in what is almost downtown Myrtle Beach.

That is how much major development has come to the area surrounding The Hill. The Hill is just a little way up from Broadway at the Beach and the Pelicans baseball stadium. The Pelicans are an Atlanta Braves "High Class A" minor league team that has produced some good baseball players that are now in the major leagues. Development has displaced some of the smaller long time little communities in the area, but progress marches on in this 21st century. In the midst of all the changes and development I still think of the good old days and how calm and peaceful things were all over the area. Some of the big name stars that stopped by The Hill on their way to Florida from the northeast also stopped at McKenzie Beach, a little farther down highway 17.

McKenzie Beach (Magnolia Beach)
A Resort That Faded Away

McKenzie Beach was also a Black beach resort that was located about 25 miles south of Myrtle Beach off highway 17 on the Waccamaw Neck. It was a barrier island as it was located between the Atlantic Ocean and the mainland, and was connected to the mainland by a causeway. McKenzie Beach was also known as Magnolia Beach in the 1930's when it was organized or developed around 1934, etc. It too was born out of segregation and offered Black tourists and travelers a place to stay on their long journey up and down the Carolina Lowcountry. It was located between Pawleys Island and Litchfield Beach, and some of the big name stars that played on The Hill in Myrtle Beach also played and stayed at McKenzie Beach as they were traveling through the area.

McKenzie Beach had lodging and restaurants, bars, etc. and was booming and going strong until that monster of a hurricane called "Hurricane Hazel" hit the area in 1954, and completely devastated the area, including the beach. The oceanfront property lines were rearranged, and the small causeway leading from the beach to the mainland was destroyed.

It appears that the owner or remaining partner took out a mortgage in an attempt to rebuild. The mortgage was foreclosed on, and in any event the resort failed and fell into disrepair over the decades. It now appears that major development is coming to the area, and the beach will be developed once again. Ways of life come and go, especially the good life and good old times full of history just fades away, but remain in our memories.

These once small pocket communities fall to development, as there is a tremendous demand for beachfront properties on all coasts. When Hurricane Hazel hit I was still in elementary school, and was spending my summers on Sandy Island at that time. I never got the opportunity to visit McKenzie Beach as it no longer existed during the years that I was visiting Atlantic Beach. I often went through Brookgreen Gardens, just up from McKenzie Beach, on my way to Sandy Island from my home in Conway.

Conway, an Old Historic Riverfront Town

Conway is an Old Historic Riverfront Town along the Waccamaw River here in this part of the southeast. It was founded around 1734 and settled around 1735 and has a deep history. It is the county seat of Horry County, the county in which Myrtle Beach is located. Myrtle Beach is known the world over as a major tourist attraction with its many beaches and resorts up and down the Grand Strand Area. Conway is perhaps one of the best kept secrets in the area as it sits about 14 miles slightly northwest of Myrtle Beach.

Conway has not yet been developed to the extent that the Myrtle Beach Grand Strand Area has been developed. But major development is coming to Conway and it is continuing to grow, and if you're coming into town from Myrtle Beach on highway 501 it's sometimes difficult to know where Myrtle Beach ends and Conway begins.

The Gullah communities in Conway still reside in the same communities when I was growing up there in the 1950's. We still have the Race Path Community and the Whittemore community, even though Whittemore High School no longer exists. I still stroll through the Race Path Community with its old moss laden oak trees and historic churches, even though the old Cherry Hill Baptist Church was demolished in 2005. I stand at the corner where it once stood, and reflect on the history that it had for generations of people. The old Bethel A.M.E. church still stands just a block up the avenue. Race Path Avenue is still the focal point for many events, and I still get my haircut at the barber shop on Race Path Avenue from a childhood neighbor.

The barber is a friend of mine and we both grew up in the Baggetts Heights neighborhood. He worked and lived in the northern cities for many decades, and returned home to retire where his roots are, just as so many of us are now doing. The re-migration back to the south is one of the continuing events that will ensure that the Gullah communities and its history keeps marching on and remain alive to be taught to future generations. Many of us grew up here with little more than each other, but we went on to be successful, self sufficient and productive citizens.

We did not just sit around and complain about hardships and how few opportunities there were for us back then. We just migrated away to jobs and opportunities until it was time for us to return to our roots. I always knew that there was a timeline for all things to be done and that it was not my timeline; but it was the only Timeline that matters as it was from a higher source.

Conway and the area have changed greatly over the decades with opportunities for those who are prepared. We all face challenges in our journey through life, and we can face such challenges and succeed and make life and living better for all we have had the opportunity to come in contact with. It's wonderful being here in this part of the Carolina Lowcountry, as I'm also very close to that isolated island with no bridges, and it's still the same old Sandy Island that I remember and had so many good experiences growing up here.

The Old Historic Riverfront Town's City Hall
and Marina are among its many historic sites

The old back yard settings were a sight to
behold back in the old days and it's still where
we call home sweet home

Old moss laden oak trees are still a landmark all
over town and some old tobacco barns can be
seen on the landscape

The old Horry County Courthouse still stands
even though a new courthouse is now right
behind it

Sandy Island – A Pristine Isolated Island

Sandy Island has been home to the Gullah people for centuries, and was settled during post reconstruction by a group of freedmen. The island is isolated and there are no bridges to the island, and it has remained virtually unchanged for centuries, even though the homes now have all the modern conveniences of life. The homes there now have electricity, water, televisions, telephones, computers, internet, etc. But, when you step out of your house there are no paved streets and the same old sandy roads and sandy pathways are there that have been there for centuries. There are still no public facilities on the island, no stores, no shops, no restaurants, no police stations, no fire stations, and no government offices, etc. The isolation has helped the Gullah people retain their unique culture that was passed down to them by the residents of West Africa who were involuntarily brought to these shores centuries ago to work as slaves.

There are a number of old rice plantations in the area near the Waccamaw Neck, and some are now open for tourists with guided tours. Sandy Island lies just across the mighty Waccamaw River, one of the few black water rivers in the world. The slaves on the old rice plantations produced some of the best rice in the world at that time, it was so good it was called "Waccamaw Gold" and some of it was exported to Europe. I had the experience and pleasure of spending the summers on the island when I was young growing up. My father was born and raised on this isolated island, and my roots are deeply embedded there. I spent many days going across the Waccamaw River going to the Gullah settlements on the eastern side of the island.

The Great Pee Dee River surrounds the island on the west side, and across the Great Pee Dee River is the little country town called Plantersville where my mother was born and raised. The Gullah People on Sandy Island today are direct descendants of the Gullah People who organized the first settlements on the island. They reside there, not too far from the banks of the Waccamaw River just as so many generations have before them.

Development has not come to the isolated island, even though there were past attempts; and now that a little over 75% of the island is owned by the state of South Carolina, development is not coming at this time. The state purchased the island to preserve it for the people of South Carolina, and its wetlands and natural pristine beauty will be preserved for the people of South Carolina. The eastern quarter of the island is privately owned by homeowners, etc. and that is where the Gullah people reside in three settlements. Many still occupy the land passed down to them from their ancestors, and still carry on the traditions of the Gullah people.

There are no bridges to the isolated island and the residents must park their cars at the Sandy Island Landing and take their motor boats across the Waccamaw River to get to their homes on the island. With no development in sight the island will remain as it has for centuries, virtually unchanged and in its pristine and natural beauty. History and memories are deep and abound all over the Gullah settlements-villages on the island. I have heard stories of the old plantations in the area all up and down the Waccamaw Neck. The river narrows somewhat as it passes and resembles a long neck and it goes a little farther south. There are stories and memories of the old graves in the area, some are covered deeply by brush and time after so many years of neglect, and hidden way back off the beaten trails.

Sandy Island is about the only major Gullah area on or near the Myrtle Beach Grand Strand area that has not been developed, or is in the plans to be developed. It is in Georgetown County, a different county from where Atlantic Beach is in, as Atlantic Beach is located in Horry County. Georgetown is south of Horry County and McKenzie Beach was located in Georgetown County. As you go south on highway 17 leaving Myrtle Beach and going to Georgetown you will pass other little communities and beach areas, some of which still have some small Gullah pocket communities. These are places such as, Murrells Inlet, Pawleys Island, Burgess, Socastee, etc.

Murrells Inlet, Pawleys Island, Burgess, Socastee
Some of the Gullah people migrated from Sandy Island to other little communities on the Waccamaw Neck and nearby to work and live. Murrells Inlet and Pawleys Island are barrier islands along the Waccamaw Neck. The oceanfront side of the islands, east of highway 17 has been developed with many oceanfront hotels, condominiums, resorts, etc. for the tourists and locals alike. The small Gullah communities are farther away from the oceanfront, on the west side of highway 17. Burgess and Socastee are a little bit away from the ocean, and were small country towns where some of the children resided who were my classmates in high school.

Some of my old high school classmates still reside in the areas, with development all around, and a way of life that once was a-fading. These smaller Gullah pocket communities still exist not too far from the major developments, and the people are continuing to carry on

29

the traditions of their Gullah ancestors in these smaller communities. This is expected as many of them still spend a large amount of their time on the Sea Islands visiting their families and friends who still reside on the nearby islands. Some still reside on land they inherited from their ancestors, but many also acquired their land by hard work and commitment just as their ancestors did so many years ago. It is also very encouraging to see so many of the younger generation in these pocket communities become self sufficient and independent by hard work.

All cultures are "very good" (Genesis 1:31). In the study of history and culture, as you get deeper into the history there is always an economic lesson embedded there. If you would just pause and reflect a little, you would see clearly that our ancestors succeeded with a lot less than we have today; and that is true of all cultures. All people and cultures also face a same fundamental economic challenge today, that is, we must all adapt to the changing economies and be prepared to compete in the global economy, no matter where we reside. We all must adapt to this highly technological 21st century society we now live in. Major economic events in the global economy will affect you in your little local economy, no matter where you live. We must all study and work, and acquire the economic skills that are needed in the global economy, as these skills are also needed in the national and local economies. If you preserve your heritage and know your history, you will see the economic lessons that will enable you to be prepared to compete in the changing society as we move deeper into this highly technological 21st century society. Our ancestors succeeded with a lot less than we have today, and we too can succeed with what we have today as we approach the critical crossroads of our sojourn here.

The Sandy Island Landing is where the residents park their cars and get into their boats to go across the Waccamaw River to get home on Sandy Island

They just get into their small motor boats and go
merrily on their way to the isolated island they
have called home for generations

The Prince Washington is the Sandy Island
school boat and it is the only school boat owned
by the State of South Carolina

The old Sandy Island School educated many
generations for decades and still stands as a
wonderful memory

Children had to walk these old sandy roads from
Annie Village and Georgia Hill all the way to
Mount Arena to go to the old Sandy Island
School rain or shine.

To go to high school they had to take the school
boat across the Waccamaw River to the Sandy
Island Landing and take a school bus to Howard
High School in Georgetown.

Georgetown's Gullah Communities

As you continue on down Highway 17 south past Pawleys Island on The Waccamaw Neck you will soon get to Georgetown, the largest town in Georgetown County and the third oldest city in South Carolina. It was founded about 1730, about five years before Conway in Horry County. The Gullah children that lived on Sandy Island went to high school at Howard High School in Georgetown during the 1950's. The children on Sandy Island would take the school boat from their island and come across the Waccamaw River to the Sandy Island Landing, and then they would have to take a school bus another fifteen miles or so to get to school in Georgetown. This was a daily occurrence rain or shine, and it was bad in the rain walking on those sandy roads on the island.

There are also some smaller pocket communities near Georgetown, such as Plantersville, where my mother was born and raised. I had often heard of stories of how many of the children in these smaller country towns had to walk miles to get to their little two to four room little schools. They were happy just to have any type of school, and in some cases where there were no schools, the teachers in these little communities had classes in their homes or in the churches.

Georgetown has always been a big center for the Gullah people, and their achievements in the town and beyond are very well known. They have a very good Gullah museum in town and have various events to keep the culture and history alive. The first Black United States Congressman was from Georgetown, and his name was **Joseph Hayne Rainey.** His portrait now hangs in the

United States Capitol, it was unveiled in 2005 over one hundred years after he died. He was born a slave in 1832 here in Georgetown, and elected a United States Congressman in 1870, and died in 1887 and is buried here in Georgetown. The Rice Museum in Georgetown has a display on Joseph Hayne Rainey, and the museum also has a display on Gullah history. There is quite a bit of Gullah history in the area, and major development has not gotten here yet as it has on the Myrtle Beach Grand Strand area.

There are also a number of old plantations around the area that have a lot of Gullah history from the days of slavery. Old plantations such as, Hampton, Hobcaw Barony, and Hopseewee Plantation, and others are here near historic Georgetown near the Sampit River. The rice production on these old plantations was once the main economy for the area. There are historic tours offered by some of the old plantations, and there are some old slave cabins and cemeteries on the grounds. History abounds all over the area, and many locals and tourists alike keep coming back to see and learn more about the area's history and way of life.

A good knowledge of one's culture and heritage has a way of making you want to achieve and become self sufficient and independent, just like our ancestors. Therefore it is imperative that we of the older generation keep doing all that we can to preserve and pass down the history to the younger generation. This will help insure that they too, when fully informed of their past will also strive in the spirit of their ancestors to succeed, and become self sufficient and independent. The youth of today face many distractions, and they are bombarded with so much information that some of them stray in directions that are not very productive for them.

It is apparent that some of them can't properly separate the good information from the other information or misinformation that seems to mislead so many of our young people. If they truly understood their heritage and the need to preserve it they would not be dropping out of high school in such large numbers, and just hanging out and hanging about. We can help them see that they themselves are responsible for getting the economic skills that will enable them to compete in this 21st century technological society, no matter the obstacles.

When one studies how prior generations succeeded with a lot less, and with more obstacles to overcome, they too will see that they can succeed in this 21st century technological society even though things may seem bleak at times. When I can sit on my front porch on a nice morning and enjoy the quiet serenity, and look up and down my street today and see that the owners of the majority of the other houses on the block are descendants of the Gullah people who settled this street so many decades ago. Seeing this makes one appreciates even more the accomplishments of our ancestors. This is one of the things I did not see in the major cities over the years that I lived in the major cities.

It is always refreshing to come back to this area along the Carolina Lowcountry and just go all up and down the communities seeing the changes. As you go farther south of Georgetown you pass other smaller Gullah communities and nearby old plantations until you get to Charleston, a historic city in a historic area.

Charleston, a Historic City

Charleston is about sixty miles south of Georgetown, and is a very old southern historic city. It has some historic museums with colonial life, and there is also a lot of Gullah history in the area. It has been estimated that over a third of the Blacks in America can trace their entry here to the Charleston seaports. This is where many of the slave ships that came from West Africa with their human cargo dropped off the Gullah people. There are archives in the city, and also the old slave marts and pest houses in the area.

Charleston is a large city along the Carolina Lowcountry and is where some of the Gullah people came to live and work. They came from the smaller islands and communities and the surrounding counties, and some of my relatives from Sandy Island worked in Charleston many decades ago, as work was sometimes hard to get in their little communities. In the 1940's and 1950's it was easier for them to get plenty of certain types of work, such as, brick masons and carpentry or work in the contracting field as laborers. Some of their children have now completed much and achieved because they saw what their parents were doing to make it better for them to have a better life.

These are stories that I heard since I was very young, and I also saw examples of such hard work. My father worked for a time at the shipyards in Wilmington, N.C. during the war years, as these jobs paid more back then, even though it was hard work. I remember the sacrifices they made, and I remember standing in line with my mother during the war years while she got her portion of meat at the meat store, the war affected everyone.

They had coupons as meat was rationed here in the town we were living in, as certain things were being rationed because of the war. After seeing this it made me appreciate even more the struggles that everyone had to endure during those war years. The Gullah people being on their little isolated islands were in a sense required to be self sufficient and independent if they were to survive. My visits to Sandy Island was after the war years and the people were still self sufficient and independent raising their live stocks, such as, cows, hogs, goats, chicken, etc.

After the war some of the people from the smaller communities returned to Charleston to work in certain fields, such as brick masons. Brick masonry was a trade they were permitted to learn and apply in those years because they needed cheap hard labor to build various buildings, etc. Charleston has always been a special city.

A branch of **The Freedman's Bank** was located in Charleston, and bank records show that some freed slaves placed money in the bank during the late 1860's and early 1870's. The bank failed in 1874 due to fraud and mismanagement, and over $57 million of freedmen's money was gone. The Freedman's Bank was organized in 1865 by Congress to help the freedmen; the bank's headquarters was in Washington, D.C. with 37 branch offices in 17 states and the District of Columbia.

Charleston is also a major tourist area and not too far from the Myrtle Beach Grand Strand area. The Gullah people are active in the city, and have preserved the history and culture. History is all around the area and as you go farther south there is Beaufort County, St. Helena Island, Hilton Head Island and Daufuskie Island among others.

Beaufort County
St. Helena Island – The Penn Center

Beaufort County is the focal point for many of the Gullah events and activities held throughout the year. Beaufort County has been home to Gullah communities for centuries, and the Penn Center is located on St. Helena Island in Beaufort County. The area is dedicated to preserving the Gullah culture and heritage, and there are historic tours that one can take to get a better understanding of the deep history here.

There are a number of Sea Islands in the Carolina Lowcountry area around Beaufort and Charleston with a lot of history to tell over the decades and centuries. It was on St. Helena Island that some of the first schools for freed slaves were established. These schools are on the site of The Penn Center, a very historic place full of Gullah history. The Praise House is also on site, and it was a house of worship for slaves built in 1840. The Penn Center is one of the Reconstruction sites in Beaufort County, and is instrumental in preserving the Gullah culture and history. For decades very little has been taught with respect to reconstruction, and it is imperative that the history of the Gullah culture is taught and preserved.

The Penn Center has an extensive archive of centuries of Black history. When The Penn Center could no longer afford to house such extensive records because of a lack of storage space, they wanted such records to be archived at the University of South Carolina in 1962. The University of South Carolina would accept the collection but wouldn't allow "equal access" as they were still a segregated university at that time down here.

The University of North Carolina at Chapel Hill was integrated and accepted The Penn Center collections, and such collections remain at the University of North Carolina to this day. The University of North Carolina has a very extensive Southern Historical Collection.

A tremendous amount of history is available here in this part of the southeast, and it is just wonderful to have the excess time to see it or research it or take tours around the historical grounds, etc. And we who have lived it and now have the time to reflect back on much more than we were taught in the schools growing up; and here is our opportunity to record all this wonderful history with facts to impart knowledge of this which is beneficial to everyone. For without knowing the truth we will not be free, for it really is the truth that can make you free. A good knowledge of one's culture and heritage will go a long way in helping to solve some of the major problems facing some of our neighborhoods today.

Hilton Head Island
The Freedmen's Village at Mitchellville

As I was growing up here in the 1950's I often heard of Hilton Head Island, although I didn't get a chance to visit it then. I knew it was sort of a Gullah focal point with Gullah activities during the year. In fact, Hilton Head Island was a predominantly Gullah community many decades ago, and the Gullah people lived off the land and waters, and many of them made their livelihood by fishing, especially shrimp fishing. Hilton Head Island was accessible only by ferry until the mid 1950's, and the old way of life thrived.

But development came and a way of life became threatened. A bridge came to the island, and a bridge to such an island inevitably means big time development with a lot more people a-coming with very different lifestyles. This means that land and living on the island will become more expensive, even for the people who've lived there all their lives living primarily off the land, and calling this place home. The local residents did not totally foresee all the major changes that were about to come to their little hide away island, but such changes were already on the drawing board.

The bridge came and major development came with it, and Hilton Head Island is now a wealthy resort with condominiums, golf courses, etc. A few people living off the land is now replaced by major development with over 50,000 new residents. Times change and development is a step in the progress ladder, as demands for more resorts grow even greater. The Sea Islands have always been choice areas for development with their quaint isolated locations.

As long as a demand exists for such resorts the major developers will continue to meet and supply that demand. Very few if any of the local Gullah people could afford to live in such wealthy resorts after they have been developed. Therefore, they pulled back and moved to other Gullah communities and continued to keep the culture and history alive. We have examples of the shifting Gullah areas as more people are forced to relocate to the mainland from the islands they once called home for generations.

The First Freedmen's Village
Part of our history will always remain on this island, such as; the first freedmen's village was established here in Mitchellville on Hilton Head Island. Another such island that saw major lifestyle changes is Daufuskie Island.

Daufuskie Island - Gullah Communities Gone

Daufuskie Island is also not too far from Charleston and is another example of what happens when development comes to an island accustomed to a certain type of lifestyle. Development displaces many long time residents of communities including Gullah residents, and destroys old ways of life. The Gullah community and culture strived on Daufuskie Island for generations as it was undeveloped with no bridges to the island. There is still no bridge to the island, but there is a ferry service to and from the island. The school boat is owned and operated by a private contractor.

When there was no major development on the island the Gullah community was thriving with over 60 families on the island they called home. In the mid 1980's major development came to the island, and now the Gullah families on the island can be counted on one hand, as there are less than a half dozen Gullah families on the island. As more and more development came they found that they were not able to afford to continue to live in such high cost living areas.

Development brought condominiums, golf courses, tennis courts, paved roads, and a luxury resort community with a good life for those who can afford such a lifestyle. Development always brings in things that the natives don't want, can't afford, or need with their way of life; and therefore they become displaced. Another historical problem is that the prior generations eschewed wills, and there were multiple owners of some Gullah land, and some developers exploited the problem by offering a fraction of owners a good price for their ownership percentage, eventually forcing court sales (leveraged sales). This is and was a problem not unique to any one island or place, but was common wherever there was choice land needed for development.

As they say progress marches on and we all should be prepared to take advantage of opportunities in this highly technological 21st century global economy. That may be easier said than done for many people as there may be a natural tendency to remain in one's own quiet lifestyle. Major development is still occurring all over this area and will continue to occur, and we must be prepared for it. As we relocate to preserve our culture and heritage in new communities, some of our culture is left behind in our old communities; but we must move on and keep our light a-shining.

The Gullah cemeteries are left behind in these resort communities. There are many such old cemeteries along the Carolina Lowcountry, and along resorts on the Waccamaw Neck, and in Brookgreen Gardens, as well as the Mary Field cemetery on Daufuskie Island. A significant part of our Gullah culture and heritage remain in these resort areas in the form of old cemeteries, in areas that we can no longer afford to live in. Some old plantations are now historic sites and offers tours to tourists and locals alike, so we can at least visit our old Gullah cemeteries in the communities we once called home. A significant part of us still reside there, on those old Lowcountry Sea Islands and beyond.

We shall keep moving on to a new day even though major development is still a-coming, and other Gullah land may become lost to even more demand for choice resort areas near the ocean. It often pains me to see the lost of so much land and communities of long ago gone, and converted to luxury resorts.

Some of the new suburbs not too far from the Myrtle Beach Grand Strand area beaches were old country communities a few decades ago. I used to work on some of the farms outside of Conway during the summertime when I was a teenager to get extra money for school clothes. Some of my classmates at Whittemore High School in Conway lived and worked on farms as their parents were farmers. I never in my wildest dreams saw or thought that these country communities in these backwoods would one day be choice real estate just a few decades later.

Some of those families I knew back then remained on their land over the decades, even though small farming became a thing of the past. Some of them will have excess land for development, and must march on with the changing times. There is incredible history all over the area, and it is interesting to see how the 21st century technology has altered our lifestyles. I spent the majority of my working life in the 20th century technology; before computers in workplace, no electronic banking, no credit cards, no ATM machines, no cell phones, no internet, etc. I have seen a lot of history evolve right before my eyes, and history still abounds all over the area.

Our history is a history of struggle and
achievement and our history abounds all over

History Abounds All Over
Old Plantations, Villages, Churches

A very deep history abounds all over the Carolina Lowcountry, and time has created a natural artistic preservation of many artifacts, old cemeteries, schools, isolated villages, etc. There are a number of heritage sites in many areas and guided tours are available in many instances.

Old cemeteries are in the areas, some way back in the woods and off the beaten trails, and some almost lost by time. Some have been destroyed or bulldozed over, as some were in unmarked graves, and there was a lack of records from some of the early years. There is a foundation in the state that is dedicated to finding and preserving the old Black cemeteries lost or forgotten.

I remember some old cemeteries from back in the 1950's, and each time I visited the area over the decades I tried to go and visit some of the areas with the old cemeteries. We played baseball in the 1950's in a wooded area near an old cemetery. Over the decades the area became more developed, and now houses are near the old cemetery there in Taylor Square. The old cemetery is still there with a little less overgrowth now, but still not well kept, it's like time has forgotten that it is there.

I remember going to funerals in the early 1950's on Sandy Island and Plantersville to bury my relatives in the old cemeteries. On Sandy Island there were no vehicles in those days, so they used a cart-wagon pulled by an ox (oxen cart) as a hearse to carry the casket from the big house to the church and old cemetery.

We marched behind the oxen cart and casket all the way from the big house to the church over a mile away for the funeral. Some of those old cemeteries in those isolated areas may be hard to find now, and some of those old cemeteries are now on land that was sold to new owners. To get to some of the old cemeteries we must go on land now owned by someone else, even though back in those old days the land was owned by our ancestors.

Old plantations are in the area and some of the old cemeteries are on the old plantations. Brookgreen Gardens (Millbrook) have some old cemeteries or slave burial grounds back in the woods, and they have guided tours through the area. Brookgreen Gardens was the site of four plantations on the Waccamaw Neck where the slaves worked the rice fields. They worked and buried their dead in the area, and there are many unknown slave graves there in the woods. Some of the old plantations there were, Springfield Plantation, Laurel Hill Plantation, and the Oaks Plantation with the Alston Cemetery, named after its owner.

Slave funerals were always on Sunday nights when they were not working. There are undoubtedly an untold number of old cemeteries with unmarked graves out there in the woods that have overgrown, and are now hidden by marshes, and watched over by the old moss laden live oak trees. There are people and a foundation in the state dedicated to identifying and restoring old grave sites. There are groups working to preserve the old cemeteries as major development is continuing to come to areas we have always considered sacred. Some of the graves may be unmarked or unknown, but their sacrifices will never be forgotten. They worked the old rice plantations on the Waccamaw Neck and beyond.

Old Plantations – Many generations were here before us and made great sacrifices and their handiworks can be seen today on some of the old plantations, in the magnificent buildings, etc. that they built. From about the early 1800's to about the beginning of the 1900's Blacks were a majority in this area, and worked the fertile lands of the Lowcountry and the old rice plantations. Some of the old plantations along the Waccamaw Neck were, Pipe Down, Taylor Hill, Blain, Oak Lawn, Oak Hampton, Sandy Knowe, Ruinsville, Laurel Hill, The Oaks, and Springfield. Other notable old plantations in the area that are now tourist attractions are as follows.

Hampton Plantation – An old rice plantation with old rice fields, and is located in McCellanville, about 15 miles southwest of Georgetown. Hampton Plantation is a state historic site and a national historic landmark.

Boone Hall Plantation – is located in Mount Pleasant, near Charleston. Some of the 9 original slave cabins have been restored and are on the Avenue of the Oaks, and can be seen when you take a tour.

Hobcaw Barony – is off highway 17 near Georgetown, it is now a research and reserve, and tours can be made by advance reservation as public access is limited. It was once the home of 14 plantations located between the Waccamaw River and the Atlantic Ocean. **Friendfield Village,** a 19th century slave village is located here, and there is a church in which the slaves and their descendants worshipped. This is the only existing slave village on the Waccamaw Neck.

Hopseewee Plantation – is located near highway 17 south of Georgetown. It is the site of an old rice plantation, and is a state historic site, and a national historic landmark. There are original slave cabins on the grounds and tours are available. Thomas Lynch Jr. a signer of the Declaration of Independence once lived on this old plantation.

There is a tremendous amount of Gullah history all over the Carolina Lowcountry and beyond, including the upstate. I have always been fascinated about what I saw and visited when I was growing up here in the 1950's, although some of the old plantations were off limits to us then. I knew that our ancestors made it better for us today, and proof is here in me recording the history of this area from my perspective and vantage point. Everyone's culture is very good (Genesis 1:31) and I am thankful that I have the opportunity to come back and record some aspects of the Gullah culture and heritage, that was extremely beneficial to me as I traveled throughout the country over the past half century. I know that a good knowledge of one's culture and heritage is essential to happiness and progress.

The old plantations are very historic and retain a lot of history, and that is attested to by the fact that so many people are going there now on the many tours that are offered. The old plantation houses and monuments are today a living legacy and tribute to the skills of the West African slaves who built such monuments and buildings on these historic plantations. The West African slaves were also very skilled in producing abundant rice crops, and knew the intricacies of good rice production. This area produced the second greatest (China first) rice culture in the history of the world. The rice crop in the area here was known as Waccamaw Gold, and was exported to Europe. Some small scale rice production continued until into the 1940's in some isolated areas.

52

There are many artifacts, some undiscovered still on the old rice plantations, especially in and around the old slave graveyards and villages. All up and down the Waccamaw Neck today you can see the skills of the Gullah people in the big estates and monuments that were constructed with free labor. Gullah labor was used to help build Brookgreen Gardens with its magnificent outdoor sculptures. The Atalaya House at Huntington Beach State Park was built with a lot of Gullah labor. The Gullah men were trained as brick masons to help build Brookgreen Gardens and Atalaya House at Huntington Beach State Park. These are still some of my favorite spots to visit, especially the Huntington Beach State Park.

I remember my uncle and my father's cousins from Sandy Island working as brick masons, and my uncle helped build the old brick Whittemore High School in Conway in the 1940's. In fact he even stayed with us in Conway part of the time he was working on the school. I was very proud going to a lovely old brick school knowing that my uncle had helped build such a wonderful brick school. The Gullah people of the prior generation really prided themselves in being hard workers to become self sufficient and independent.

In the Gullah communities all up and down the Carolina Lowcountry, including the smaller pocket communities, the people still take pride in being self sufficient and independent. Although it's more difficult now for many people because development has altered or displaced a way of life in some communities, and it is more difficult now to just live primarily off the land and rivers and ocean. Change has been difficult for many, but we all must adapt to change in our lives and communities in this 21st century highly technological society.

Changing Times - Our ancestors were able to live off the land and waters in some of the surrounding isolated areas and Sea Islands decades ago in the prior century. Life was a lot slower and calmer then and many rural families could earn a living on the small family farms. And even though some of our ancestors had to start out as sharecroppers, they eventually were able to own their own land through hard work and perseverance. It must have been very difficult being a sharecropper in those days, knowing that you had to work from virtually sunrise to sunset in order to make a living and feed your family, because a percentage of the harvest was owed to the landowner in the big house. That generation succeeded because they had to come from such a long way from the bottom, and made the necessary sacrifices in order to have a better day.

We too have succeeded and have come a very long way with many achievements. Our past has taught us a very profound lesson that we can never forget. But our true success can only be measured in how far we have come in our lifetime. Some people are born into wealth and privilege, but we were not. Some people started out with good jobs in the corporate world, but we did not. Some people had all types of job opportunities when they graduated from school, but most of us had very limited job opportunities in the 1950's and 1960's when we finished school, but we marched on to take advantage of what little opportunities we had.

But we took advantage of the opportunities that were available to us, and worked our way up and into better jobs and positions in the workplace. Just think of where we may have ended up if we had started out at the same place as those with wealth or privilege. So if you were to measure success by how far a person has come, and what they had to overcome, you too will see and agree that we were very successful and made a great contribution to life and society, and left a better path for subsequent generations to follow. Many of us came from the very bottom and rose way above the water line, for we knew that the river was rising; and we competed and succeeded against many who started out above the water line. We were a generation of struggle, but we succeeded and made it with the help and Grace of God!

A Deep South Generation of Struggle – A Migration Away and a Remigration Back – We were truly a generation of struggle and the history of the country reflects that for those who care to seek the truth. A generation born into little or no economic opportunities in our home states, and where it took many marches and sit in demonstrations just to obtain certain basic rights in society. Many of us had no choice except to migrate away to get a job and a higher education. We were also a migration generation, but no matter where we went, to the northeast or out west, we were determined to excel.

In all the years we were away from our roots, we never forgot where we came from. And even though we started out a little farther back than most of our co-workers in the workplace, it didn't take us long to surpass most of our co-workers. They never could figure out or fully understand why we were such hard workers and determined to succeed. But we knew that he who starts out with less must run faster and work harder to get even and forge ahead in society. This was instilled in us in our upbringing and is part of our roots, as we saw that our parents became self sufficient and independent by hard work and a deep and abiding faith in God. This was a trademark of our down home communities, and the way life was back down home.

Even though most of us migrated away to far away cities and states to get better opportunities, we took with us a commitment to return and make life here in the communities we were reared in even better. We also were committed to making life better in the communities that we were residing in all those years we were away. We knew that we had to remain committed to our goals and objectives in order to achieve them. Our Deep South roots in the Gullah communities we were reared in gave us a good foundation upon which to build on even though we were far from home.

We established priorities and were committed to getting ahead by continuing our education and acquiring Economic Skills (not just degrees). We knew from just observing life in our Gullah communities that our parents' generation had acquired a measurable degree of self-sufficiency and independence by acquiring Economic Skills that were needed in the marketplace. This also enabled them to obtain ownership of some of the businesses in their communities. The Gullah communities had their own motels, lodges, etc. in some of the communities when I was growing up here in the 1950's. We now have more degrees but less ownership of the businesses that we once owned that was located right within our communities.

Life in the communities was different from what it is today. Four or five decades ago the Gullah communities were a lot smaller and everyone knew everyone, so to speak, or at least knew all the families in the community. Most of us went to the same high school in Conway, as the old Whittemore High School was the only high school in the county that we could attend in those days, and children came here from far and wide from all the outlying towns and country communities.

We lived in Conway on a dirt road that wasn't paved, and when it rained a lot the road became muddy in spots, and cars would get stuck in the mud. We moved into our new house on the dirt road in 1946, and the road wasn't paved when I migrated away in 1961. I migrated away to California to further my education and make a better living, as opportunities for us were limited or non-existent to us in those days. I knew that if I had made it through those days there on that dirt road that I would maintain the fortitude to make it farther and succeed.

The city life was good in those old days, and our little big communities were more closely knitted than they are today. Many of us in our city communities had migrated from various southern states to make a better living. This was the 1960's, before drugs and other untold mind twisters were introduced into the communities. Many of us even brought our Southern Bible Belt lifestyles to the big cities. The first baseball team I played on in the city was with church guys mostly from Texas and Louisiana. We even had a preacher playing on our baseball team part time as a substitute player as he couldn't make it to all our games. Those were some good old days and we were able to enjoy our Bible belt communities in the cities. But like everything else, things change over time and a new generation emerged on the timeline.

The same is true all along the Gullah communities on the Carolina Lowcountry in all the counties and their pocket communities. There is an untold number of Gullah pocket communities in these counties too numerous to mention. My home county of Horry has many smaller places and towns, such as, Wampee, Popular, Aynor, Gallivants Ferry, Loris, Homewood, and many other smaller Gullah outlying communities on rural routes, etc.

57

Many of us have now returned to our communities amid so much change and development. Some of the communities nearer the coast or Atlantic Ocean no longer exist, as they have been developed for the tourist market. Land that was once traditional Gullah communities and farmlands near the coast is now occupied by condominiums, golf courses and modern resorts.

There are still some major Gullah communities away from the coast or Atlantic Ocean. Conway is just fourteen miles slightly northwest of Myrtle Beach, and there are various events in town and around the area. The Myrtle Beach area is a major focal point for the many family reunions during the year, especially during the summer and holidays. It's a different mix now with multiple generations residing in the communities now because times have changed significantly for the younger generation. Today the young generation is greatly influenced by television with its' many x rated programs, and some of the youngsters emulate such lifestyles, hip hop, etc.

This makes it even more imperative that we pause, reflect, and take a committed approach to making sure that our communities keep passing on the Gullah culture and heritage to subsequent generations in the midst of these special changing times. We were reared with a different value system decades ago, and it was such a value system that enabled us to continue on and succeed, and reach our goals and objectives in spite of obstacles along the way. Now in the neighborhoods that remain the younger generation have a different mindset, and many are influenced by various happenings in the larger environment that impacts their little communities.

Our history in the area goes deep, from our small country stores to the rivers and boat docks way back on our pristine isolated islands

Our ancestors were here centuries ago and were
laid to rest in many of the old cemeteries way
back in the rural areas we once called home

It was here in these small towns that they
worked hard so that their children could get a
good education at the local schools such as, the
old Whittemore High School

They established their churches right here in the communities and some were founded over a century ago, the church has always been the main institution in our communities

In the isolated communities the people looked
out for each other and the communities were
tightly knitted on these isolated pockets

Throughout the decades and centuries as many changes has occurred the people keep marching on and hanging on to their heritage and culture

Same Neighborhoods – Subsequent Generations

I constantly roam through many neighborhoods taking in the changes, and even though many neighborhoods are the same as they were decades ago, new generations are residing there along with what's left of the older generation. Many of the younger generation have a different mindset and some are headed in other directions. My old neighborhood has remained virtually unchanged for many decades; some of the same families are still there in the same houses as when I was growing up there in the 1950's. It's the subsequent generations that are the majority there now, in some houses it's the children of the parents who first settled there over a half century ago, and in other houses it's the children and grandchildren.

I can remember back in the 1950's when we were going to school, and it was during the summer and my parents were working. I decided that it would be a good time for me to practice smoking a cigarette. I went under our house as it had about a three foot crawl space, and lit up a cigarette or partial cigarette, as these were the days before cigarettes had filters. I don't recall where I got the cigarette from, although I may have taken one of my father's cigarettes. In any event I lit up and began to smoke the cigarette under the house knowing that my brothers and sister was in the front yard or front porch. I just kept puffing away as if all was well and feeling safe under the house.

But to my surprise my neighbor next door was sitting in her front yard under her tree enjoying the cool breeze. I then heard her say she smelled smoke, and then she asked my brothers and sister if they were cooking anything, or knew where the smoke was coming from. It was then and there that I tried to hold in the big puff that I had just taken. I was almost about to cough when I heard her ask, now where is Thomas. There was silence, and all I know is that I somehow got rid of that big puff without coughing too loudly. I then gently went around the other side of the house to the front yard so I could be seen with clean hands. That was my first and last experiment with trying to learn how to smoke cigarettes, and to this day I have never been a cigarette smoker.

In those days the adults could and did discipline their neighbor's children if the children were engaging in inappropriate conduct. I had to obey the adults in the community just as I had to obey my parents. Our neighbors were there when we moved into our house in 1946, and different generations of the families still own the properties today.

I found it to be easier to come back here to the house that I grew up in, as it is easier to recall those events that happened here so many decades ago. It's also easier to document the past by coming back and living here in the area that holds and contains so much rich history. Many generations have had large families here, and some have never left the area to live elsewhere.

On my street just down on the next corner is a house where the family has been there for over half a century. Living in the house now is the subsequent generation, and as I sit on my front porch I can see them sitting on their front porch. It's been that way since we were all in school here in the 1950's. Some of us migrated away to work for decades, but we're back home now in our neighborhood, and it seems like we never left.

In some cases it's the third and fourth generation there today, and the little ones are still reared in the tradition of their ancestors. One of the little ones was a very smart and intelligent seven years old, and she knew the history of the neighborhood and the families that first inhabited the neighborhood. She knew that the families were very close back in those days and looked out for each other, and stated that our families have been close for generations, and that we are just like family even today.

I knew that her argument or position was not only true, but powerfully persuasive. Her mother and my mother were friends, and her mother even helped my mother when she was sick. I was still working in California and couldn't get back to be with my parents as much as I would have liked to. But it was comforting knowing that I had a good neighbor looking out for my mother, and they apparently spent many evenings sitting on our screened front porch. And now that my parents have passed, I now spend a lot of time on our nice screened front porch enjoying the peace and tranquility.

Some of the little ones in the neighborhood also wanted to come and sit on my screened front porch as they had noticed that I was the only one who sat there primarily. It took some explaining to convince them that it was not appropriate for them, especially the little girls to be sitting on porches with men. The little seven year old finally figured out a way to get two adult female chaperones to accompany her, as she was an artist and wanted to view my art works. She stated that she had given a lot of thought to what she wanted to be when she grows up. She was going to have an art company producing and selling art works to help the poor. I told her that was a wonderful idea and very unselfish of her, and that I was sure she would be very successful.

67

She stated that what she wanted to do might sound strange, but that's just because over 85% of the people don't understand us artists. I've always known that there's a lot of truth to that statement. She even suggested that I could teach some art classes in the neighborhood, as she wanted to take some more art classes. It was difficult for me to explain to her that I didn't have the extra time at the moment and that her art classes at her school was just fine and her portfolio was good. The neighborhood is a little different now that they have moved away while her mother completes military duty.

That reminds me of my days in the military over four decades ago. Even though we grew up here in the Carolina Lowcountry some of us have spent time all over the country and the world. Even today I remember my Air Force Serial Number just like I remember my social security number. I still review my military mementos often, especially looking at my DD form 214 showing my honorable discharge. My home base was right there in North Carolina, and I did serve some time in Thailand.

If there was some sort of mandatory service to country for all young people, perhaps some would have a different perspective on their outlook on life, I know they would acquire more discipline, as service to country is honorable. No matter what your position is in life, our ancestors worked hard and sacrificed so that we can have a better life today. They succeeded with a lot less that we have today, so there is no excuse for us not succeeding. Some injustices, be they real or perceived may always linger, but no people can wait for all injustices to end before they stand up, take a stand, and be productive law abiding citizens. Change is coming.

Change – But Not The Altering of Certain Characteristics in The Community

My little neighborhood and street haven't changed that much in the four decades that I was away. Most of the old houses are still there, as are the old families. I sit on my front porch and see many of the same neighbors now, and it's just that we are a little older now and hopefully a little wiser too. I always enjoyed coming home on vacations over the decades because coming to my childhood neighborhood was just like going back in time. A few of the old tobacco barns could still be seen about the countryside with bushes overgrown around them as they haven't been used in years. Just one of the old jewels that stuck out in the midst of the encroaching developments.

On my street (dirt road) when I was growing up an old man and his wife lived in the house across the road from us. He kept his mule in the stable in back, and he used his mule to plow his cornfield right beside his house, as his lot was actually a lot and a half. He also planted a cornfield in the lot right beside us and used his mule to plow that cornfield also. He occasionally would hitch his mule to his wagon and go a riding down the road on his errands. This was in the 1950's when all the surrounding roads were dirt roads. I actually got an early education in seeing a man till his land; and it is still written "that the man that tilleth his land shall have plenty of bread, but he that followeth after vain persons shall have poverty enough" (Proverbs 28:19).

That generation always worked hard, and they were very productive as there were no government handouts in those days. I constantly marvel at the things my parents

69

endured in order to support their family on limited resources. We were never in poverty and always had plenty to eat, with decent shelter here in this house which still stands today, more solid than many of the newer houses of today.

The Gullah people along the Carolina Lowcountry have always been a very resourceful people, with tremendous fortitude, and a deep faith. This is still very much a Bible belt community even though most of the older generation has died out now. You can now buy beer and wine on Sunday, as the law now allows it. But there are still some major outlets that have signs up on Sundays stating that we do not sell beer and wine on Sundays. The deep seated beliefs in such Bible belt communities are strong and transcend certain man made laws.

I will be forever grateful that I was raised in a Bible belt community among the Gullah people here in the Carolina Lowcountry. There are things that one learns in these communities that become permanently ingrained in them no matter where they go. Their faith is deep and has always been that way, and we referred to the elder generation as seven days a week true believers. They didn't just act well on Sundays; they actually practiced their faith every day. There is something different about these Bible belt communities, and I can still feel it deep, deep down within. It is doubtful that any amount of development will ever change or alter a major characteristic of these communities that is their deep and abiding faith.

A Deep Faith in These Bible Belt Communities

During these rapidly changing times due to time, development, and different generations, the communities have changed and faced new challenges. Many of the younger generation have a different agenda than their parents' generation. Some of them are intent on doing their thing their way on their own right now timeline. This does not always work in these changing times in this highly technological 21st century society. The youngsters cannot completely do it their way because they are still somewhat under the influence of the prior generation and connected to our Bible belt communities and way of life.

The prior generations worked harder with fewer resources to become self sufficient, after making many sacrifices. Their achievements and accomplishments under such adverse conditions made me a deep believer in their way of life, and I strived to retain the same deep faith and belief in God, as practiced in our Bible belt communities. Their fortitude carried them through some difficult times, and I knew that I would need the same fortitude to carry me as I left the community and migrated out west to work and study. I knew that I would one day return to my roots and carry on in the tradition of these wonderful people here in these down home communities.

We went to Sunday school and church almost every Sunday, as it was not only the main thing to do, but the only thing to do on Sundays. I enjoyed going to church in our Bible Belt Gullah community with the prior generation. I enjoyed the old time gospel singers,

71

especially the Jubilee Singers at the Bethel A.M.E. church during the 1950's. They never used music to accompany them, they just clapped their hands and patted their feet and the gospel rhythm just flowed.

The lead singer of the Jubilee Singers at the church was a cousin of mine, she was from the same little country town my mother was from, Plantersville, S.C. just in the next county south of here. They always were the main choir at least once a month, and I made sure I was at church and on time the Sunday they were singing. There was a little calm and quietness before they started singing and the lead singer would just start leading off while they all were seated. It wasn't long before they started patting their feet, and standing up clapping their hands, and every part of the rhythm was in sync. Even today I can go into my quiet study area, and close my eyes and visualize that scene today, and I'll just pat my feet as I recall those good old days of that group of Jubilee Singers.

That prior generation was a strong generation, and it was obvious to me that it was their deep faith and belief in God that kept them strong and carried them through some difficult times. I can remember when Rosa Parks sat down on the bus and refused to give up her seat. I knew that her courageous act helped made it possible for all of us to stand up and take a stand, and be committed to become successful with study and hard work. I remember some of the Gullah students sitting in cafeterias during the early 1960's, and my deep faith enabled me to stand up and be committed to be successful, because so many people had sacrificed so that we could all have a better day. We all will face critical crossroads in our sojourn throughout the land in these latter days.

72

It has been said that we all have to walk that journey by the water's edge. That we may not all have the same role to play in the master plan, but that we must all take that journey, one way or the other. I'm glad that I chose to walk it with the same deep faith and fortitude that was passed down to me from my parents. I know that my assigned role in the master plan is to currently document and record an artistic preservation through art, writings, etc. of the history of the unique Gullah people and their culture. If I can but capture a small glimpse into the customs, habits, and folkways of these unique people and their culture, I know that I will have accomplished my assigned mission.

I always knew that this day would come for me, and some may ask, how do you know; but some things you just automatically know when to do them, no one has to tell me when to sleep or eat, I just know. There are also some things we are not taught or given, and didn't receive them from or by man, we received them by revelation (Galatians 1:12). No one told me when to retire or take a vacation, the body just knows when to do certain things, I just know. If we can just pause a moment, and listen to the choir that's deep down within our conscience, we'll begin to know for sure what our role is, as we all have a role in that master plan. I am a servant of the most High God, a partaker of the promise! (Genesis 14:20, Psalm 47:1,2, 82:6, St. Mark 5:7, St. Luke 8:28, Acts 16:17, Galatians 3:29. This is a deep part of my personal faith and belief in God, and was deeply rooted in me from my days in our Bible belt communities down home.

Life here in these Carolina Lowcountry communities are still wonderful, in spite of the continuous growth and development. We've lost some parts of our little communities due to such development, but our faith throughout our Bible belt communities all up and down the Carolina Lowcountry is still strong.

I constantly travel all over the area taking in, recording, and documenting the history of my people here down home. And everywhere I go in the counties I still see the hope and deep faith of the people, even among the younger generation with all the distractions confronting them. They see that some of the communities that they grew up in are no longer their little communities, as it has been taken over by growth and development. The elder generation is constantly teaching them that the acquisition of Economic Skills will enable them to play a larger and key role and compete in the global economy. There is a little culture shock in seeing traditional Gullah neighborhoods and communities being displaced by development. The faith and fortitude of the people deep down in these neighborhoods remain strong and will enable them to make a significant contribution to the economic revitalization of their neighborhoods and communities.

Change All Over – Major development has brought some profound changes to other areas and neighborhoods also, and not just to the Gullah communities along the Carolina Lowcountry. It may only be natural for people to see their situation as the major affected area. When I see this I just look to and recall the fortitude of our ancestors who overcame so much with so little. Their deep faith kept them strong, but they also believed in hard work to become self sufficient. Hard work goes hand in hand with a deep faith, for we were told millenniums ago to Study and Work (II Timothy 2:15, I Thessalonians 4:11, II Thessalonians 3:6-12, James 2:17-26, Revelation 20:12).

A deep and abiding faith has always been a
trademark in our Bible belt communities and I
often think of the old days when I saw the
fortitude it gave to our ancestors and carried
them through some difficult times

The Historic Bethel A.M.E. Church is the
church that I attended in the 1940's and 1950's
as I was growing up in our Bible belt
community and the church still stands today

The Historic Old Cherry Hill Baptist Church
was demolished in 2005 and it no longer stands
on the corner of highway 501 and Race Path
Avenue. A Landmark gone, but not forgotten.

We referred to our little Bible belt community as the Whittemore Community, the name of the school where we had some dedicated teachers who prepared us well for the challenges we were to face. We learned to work hard to achieve our Goals and Objectives.

The Value of Work, in Addition to Faith

My faith has always been very strong, but I knew that I also had to study and work to become successful. That is something that my parents taught us and instilled in us at a very young age. When I graduated from high school my parents told me that they didn't have the money to send me to college, but that they wanted me to attend college. I knew that I would not have any trouble working my way through college in California, as college in California back then was virtually free for residents, with just a small fee.

California seemed like a good place for me to start because I loved to play baseball, and in California I could play baseball about ten months of the year while also working. This was in the days before a lot of government handouts, and where I knew that I would have to work for what I wanted. I didn't have any problems working during the day and taking college classes in the evening and at night. I knew that my hard work then would pay off later. I had seen what hard work did for my ancestors as I was growing up, and I was so proud of them being independent and self sufficient.

It has been said that you can toss a pebble into shallow water and be safe, but at some point in time one must venture out into deeper waters. One has to be more prepared when one journeys out into deeper waters, because the river is rising, and I know what happens when the river overflows. One must know when to move on up to higher ground to remain safe and receive benefits of a new day. One must be prepared as all good things don't come easy to everyone. We must plow and plant, and even though we cannot germinate the seed, we must still plow and plant in order to have a harvest. I intend to keep a crop in the ground at all times, because I need a good harvest every year. We can only plow and plant (work hard) it is a higher power that germinates the seed! We must Study and Work!

Hard or difficult times usually come into the life of everyone in one way or another, and may continue to come for a-while. But obstacles in your path to success can be overcome, it may not always be easy and sacrifices may have to be made along the way. Such sacrifices will only lead to a better day through hard work. History has clearly shown that people who do not give up and keep marching on to success will eventually triumph. Some will give up and fall by the wayside because their faith is not deeply rooted.

The influx of development has displaced not only poor people, bet it has also displaced many other working people. Many people who have lived and worked in towns or areas close to the beaches cannot now afford to live near their jobs. Many of their residences, rental units, etc. are being sold and converted to condominiums or other development. Many of the locals who've lived near the beaches for years will simply not be able to afford the post development housing prices, etc.

Major development also means many other people coming into the area to work and live, and this invariably translates into a higher cost of living in the area. Therefore, there will be a lot less affordable housing for many people who live in the area or came to the area seeking work. Hard times and difficulties come to many people and groups in the area. We must all remain focused on overcoming such obstacles in our path to make the way better for all who must come after us. Many people and groups are moving a little farther inland and acquiring land in order to remain self sufficient and independent. Some cultures are deeply rooted in the land and we need land to insure the survival of our culture. If we continue our march in a just and pragmatic direction we will see that light ahead as it shines the way to success.

Before electricity came to our little dirt road we
used kerosene lamps to keep our house lit at
night and the light kept a-shining

A Light Ahead

People who work hard to overcome obstacles and succeed will always see and remain focused on that light ahead to accomplish their goals. Many communities along the Carolina Lowcountry have been permanently altered by the changes and influx of people relocating to the area. The weather is very nice here and there are miles and miles of beaches, with a low tax rate and some affordable homes in the area. The cost of living has risen a bit but still within reach of many families relocating here who have a vision and plan to succeed.

As future retirees and the remigration continue back to the south, we should see an increase in the number of Gullah people returning to their roots to carry on in the tradition of their elders. Many of them are reaching retirement age in the cities after being away working for decades. This remigration will also help insure that the Gullah communities continue to grow and strive even in new or relocated areas. The community is where the people are and where they make it happen.

After emancipation and during post reconstruction the freed slaves relocated and started new communities and settlements. Some of these communities still exist to this day, such as, the Mount Arena community on Sandy Island, along with Annie Village and Georgia Hill on the island. The fortitude and vision of the people is what will carry them through these current profound changes in society. Although it may be a rough stretch of the road right now, it won't remain that way forever as long as we have people committed to building up, and not tearing down. Committed people can make a difference and they are not afraid to stand up and make it happen.

We Made a Difference

History has shown that my generation made a profound change and difference in our society. We were born of a generation in struggle, and we were the first generation out of struggle to get in a position to receive opportunities to get more of the economic pie that society has to offer. We took advantage of all opportunities made available to us because we knew what it was like to have nothing and to be left behind economically. We were from deep down in the hood back home so to speak, and we knew we had to earn our keeps and become highly qualified in order to compete in the economic arena offered by society at that time.

That's how it was a half century ago as we were going to school in our little communities in the Carolina Lowcountry and beyond. Life in the mid 20th century was still challenging for us, but we pushed on because we could see a light ahead and knew more opportunities awaited us. We worked through the 20th century into the highly technological 21st century, and have seen and experienced many profound changes at home and abroad. We now have instant communication with high tech electronic transfers globally, and now the current generation must also be prepared to compete in the national and global economies.

The changes in our generation have been profound and astounding, and we have met the challenges head on. Now we must make sure that the subsequent generation is well prepared to compete as they go deeper into this highly technological 21st century society. There are many more profound changes yet to come, especially with the great influx of so many people and cultures that

84

are migrating and re-migrating to the south. The south is also changing with the diversity and influx of people and cultures coming to the area.

A Changing South – New Challenges, Opportunities

Many different people from all over the country and beyond have seen something enlightening enough to make the south their new home. They are coming here from California, Hawaii and beyond, and many are coming not just to retire, but to work and live in a peaceful and tranquil new environment. Recent studies have shown that many different people of diverse backgrounds have chosen to make a new life here in the south. The Carolina Lowcountry has not just only changed in the old traditional Gullah communities, but change and development is all over the area. It's only natural that we felt a major impact here so close to our wonderful beaches, parks, rivers and waters, etc.

I know why I re-migrated back to my roots here in the south, even though I still love other areas of the country, especially the San Francisco Bay Area. But deep down I have always been a southerner, and mighty right proud of it. We cannot change the past; but, we can sure change the future and the present by standing up right here where we are and be productive in our little communities and make it better for all who are in our presence and those who will follow.

It has often been said that there are three types of people, the doers, the talkers, and the wonderers. The doers will act and be productive and be a part of progress. The talkers will only talk about what should be done or what they are doing sitting on the sidelines, but they will only talk, they will never take action and will not walk the walk. The wonderers are people who will

85

just remain on the sidelines dreaming, as they watch progress pass them by, and then they wonder what happened. The 25th Chapter of St. Matthew talks about three types of people, the wise, the foolish, and the unprofitable (nonproductive) and each group has a different mindset.

Change always brings new challenges and new opportunities for people who are prepared and have acquired the economic skills to compete in the new environment. It is a challenge that the forward thinking people of this area have always met, and I'm quite confident that they will be and remain prepared to meet the new challenges ahead. Growth also means new opportunities for those willing to work to get ahead, and the local educational systems and universities are gearing up to prepare the diverse population to take advantage of the opportunities through hard work and education. Our faith and belief is strong and has always been so, and I know that we will be prepared to succeed.

Our Priorities Must be Clear and We Must Remain Focused on Our Goals and Objectives – In many areas of the south, including our Carolina Lowcountry, there are areas and communities with large numbers of other cultures, as more people are coming to this country from other countries. There is still ample land in the southern countryside so that focused and dedicated people can still obtain some land. We cannot all afford to live near the ocean and beaches, but we can all remain focused and be productive.

We traditional southerners have always been here in spirit even when we were away working for many decades. Many different cultures are emerging now to take a more pronounced place in the southern culture.

Many of these cultures have many things in common with the southern culture, such as, being very family oriented. Many of us came from large families and extended families and grew up as just one big family.

We can all look back over time, in decades past and see communities that have changed, and are still changing if not already gone. Families with deep roots in their culture and heritage tend to stick together and adapt more easily and readily to the changing times and environment. Many people are coming here to work but will easily fall in love with the area and its' southern lifestyle, and they will make this area their home. The large numbers of people that are coming here to the area confirm that it's for real and not just a passing fad. I know that I am glad and fortunate to be able to return and reside here in the Carolina Lowcountry near the many wonderful beaches and ocean.

As I stroll down the wonderful beaches, rivers and inlets all over the Carolina Lowcountry, I often think back over time, to decades ago. I see the changes and the communities that have been altered or displaced due to time and development. We must stand up, face the facts, and seize the moment and the opportunity to be a viable part of the economic revitalization within our communities. No one will come and do for you what you should and must do for yourself. We may need to make a more concerted effort to see to it that the young people in our communities are acquiring the economic skills that will enable them to be a pragmatic part of the new renaissance within our communities. It is very easy to march down the long road to nowhere if one is not properly prepared to compete in the new environment. Going up the economic ladder will be easy for those who are willing to Study and Work to make it happen.

One must be willing to Study and Work, and put in a little extra in order to remain competitive in the society in which we now live in. That may mean extra time at the library or on-line on the internet, as information is virtually unlimited in this information age. There is a good life here in the changing Carolina Lowcountry, and it will be even better for those who are prepared to compete and be productive. That means being willing to Study and Work to maintain and upgrade your economic skills. The workplace in which I worked for over four decades was more predictable, and I started in the workplace before computers, electronic banking, etc.

I just had to come back into the workplace after I retired just to practice being competitive in this 21st century technological society. There is an awful lot that can be learned about business and industry, including the book publishing industry on-line on the internet. Research is virtually instant on the internet with a wealth of information there for those willing to Study and Work. It is very apparent to me that communities are a-changing as the new global economy is a-changing and evolving.

As the communities change I have noticed that some landmarks and what I consider to be historical community structures no longer exist and have been demolished in the name of progress. A particular old church here in my hometown no longer exist, it had stood on the same corner for well over half a century and was truly a landmark that will be sorely missed. The spot today is an empty reminder of what used to be, and as you gaze at the empty spot on the corner and think of what used to be and the many wonderful spiritual memories of years and generations long gone. We must all work to preserve that which is a deep part of us because much can and will be lost in these changes.

Preserve Your Heritage
Know Your History and Culture

It is up to each and every one of us to preserve our history and culture. Our ancestors worked hard and sacrificed so that we could have a better life, and enjoy some of the better things in life that they could not afford or were denied. They had limited opportunities but accomplished much, and left us some land in many instances. One of the major steps in preserving your culture and heritage is to preserve and upkeep the real property our ancestors passed down to us. It may be just a simple small house to many looking from the outside; but to us on the inside we know that there are many fond memories, lessons of life and history here in these few small sacred rooms. Each day I wake up I pray that I can help keep the light a-shining on their achievements during their sojourn here among us.

As I awake each morning I thank God for another day in this our historic structure we call home. I can still feel and hear their loving guidance and care here today, and each new day. We must continue to honor them, and respect them for what they accomplished, and the guidance they gave us here in this little historic structure we called home. We can do that by continuing to honor and respect their ideals, and continue to do the right thing and keep their true principles of life.

I can feel their spirit alive and well here comforting me in our little historic structure we still call home; no matter where we may have migrated to we always find our way back home. They sacrificed and gave so much so that I might be here today just enjoying the good life. It is only fitting that I continue to honor and respect

89

them, and I know that is the right and correct thing to do based on my experiences.

But that is not my only authority for honoring and respecting them: we were told to do this millenniums ago (Exodus 20: the 5th Commandment).

Precious memories can easily slip away if we keep putting off the documentation of them for a later day, for tomorrow is not promised to us. Therefore we should Study and Work to preserve and keep that which we have and is dear or sacred to us, for these are the precious memories that should be passed down to the subsequent generations.

There are many lessons to be learned in the study of one's history and culture.

A Knowledge of One's Culture and History

Can Help Solve the Major Problems in Urban Neighborhoods, etc.

- High Drop Out Rate
- High Crime Rate, etc.
- Literacy Rate Too Low
- Lack of Economic skills

Because – There are Deep Seated Economic Lessons Embedded in the Study of One's History and Culture.   Everyone's Culture is Very Good (Genesis 1:31)

But – All Cultures Face a Fundamental Economic Challenge - Must Acquire the Economic Skills to Compete in 21st Century Highly Technological Global Economy

Our Ancestors Succeeded with a Lot Less than we have today.
Consider the Economic Situation they faced – Limited Resources, Opportunities, etc.
They became Self Sufficient – Independent - Worked Land & Produced Food, etc.

Today we have unlimited access to information . . . On-Line, etc.
Unlimited Educational and Economic Opportunities - Yet a high drop out rate?

Our young students must become more cognizant of the past and how prior generations (their ancestors) worked hard to be productive in their communities. No free handouts!

We must all Study and Work to succeed and acquire the Economic Skills to compete in this Highly Technological 21st Century Society and the Global Economy.

Students have the Primary Responsibility to remain in school and become Functionally Literate!   Some of our ancestors only had 2 Room Schools.

Government is responsible for providing schools that meet certain standards.
Student is responsible for Studying and Working hard in school.

Every group in society faces obstacles in a pursuit to succeed. History teaches us this very clearly.   There is No Harvest without Plowing and Planting.

There is No Free Ride

We Have Much To Do,
and a Long Way To Go, and
There Is No Free Ride!
If Each One Does a Little; Together,
We Can Accomplish A Lot,
Injustices May Linger . . . But,
We Must Move On And Succeed in Spite of Obstacles!
Because,
We Have Much To Do,
and a Long Way To Go, and
There Is No Free Ride!

Don't Practice Economic Foolishness,
Stay in School and Get a Skill, and Be Prepared to
Compete in the Global Economic Arena! Have an
Economic Agenda!
No Economic Agenda, No Economic Autonomy.

We Have Much To Do, and a Long Way To Go, and
There is No Free Ride!

"You Can be The Head, and Not the Tail" (as stated in
Deuteronomy 28:13).
But, only "If" you fulfill the condition precedent stated
in Deuteronomy 28:13. Think and Act!

Study and Work – Acquire Land, and Develop your
Land and Obtain Economic Autonomy. (Proverbs 28:19,
12:11)

No One is Coming to Help or Save Foolish or Lazy
People. (Proverbs 26:11, 26:14, 20:4, 10:15).

Stop, and Listen . . .
Right Now;

"Let us get to the Conclusion of the Whole Matter" (as stated in Ecclesiastes 12:13).

We can enjoy the ride and have fun, but after we Study and Work

A Roaring in the Night
Restless Souls A-Wandering

I stood on my porch late that night, and it was a rainy evening all into the late night. Early past midnight the thunder began to roll and roll louder and louder. And the lightening began to dance and prance all over that moonless starless night. The roaring rain just kept on a-pouring down in buckets with the wind a-howling. Amid the torrential down-pouring, there is a sound in the distant night, a cry of the homeless scurrying for more shelter or cover as they move deeper under the overpass, and further into deeper doorways all over the mall. Some are so far out on drugs, alcohol or other untold mind-twisters that they hardly know what hit them. They're moving like fallen stars caught up in the tail of the big red dragon. Crying, crying in the waters deep, deep into that dark, dark moonless starless night, not knowing if they will make it one more hour, let alone until the coming of the morning light.

And even if they make it to the morning light, the day for them will still be dark and cloudy, and a long, long day with more crying in the waters, as they still may not make it through that long, dark and difficult day. They're so far out they just continue to linger and walk down that long road to nowhere, and the farther you walk down that long road to nowhere the longer it takes you to get back to here, here where you should have remained all along; ab initio! For there is nothing but trouble all up and down that boulevard in the danger zone, and some even calling it the killing zone.

I was cruising home at night in that danger zone when I heard a cry for a ride from a youngster. I recognized the voice, for I had given them advice before on why they must study hard to acquire economic skills. My reply was that you need a 3.5 to ride in my ride, and they responded what is a 3.5 and it was apparent to me then that they had dropped out and didn't get a passing G.P.A. I kept going and they started yelling louder and louder. You don't have to be loud and yell from the highest hill, but you must study hard and acquire economic skills, for you will need a 3.5 to ride with me in my ride.

No matter how long, dark or difficult the night may seem, just keep moving on and work for a better day, and you shall see it

Dark and cloudy days will come, but your faith
must be deep and strong and it will carry you
through that Long Day of Atonement

UNITY
A By-Product of Certain Key Ingredients

Unity is a By-Product of certain key ingredients within the community; such as, discipline, obedience, respect, economic stability, beliefs and standards, etc. Discipline may be the major ingredient because without discipline nothing else may fall in place. Children must be taught discipline at a young age, that is, they must be trained properly to develop self-control and efficiency. Children can be trained to be obedient and obey rules and regulations and exercise self-control if they know that they will receive treatment that corrects or punishes them. Discipline is a main branch of learning, and without discipline children won't be able to learn very much, and may be a disruptive force within our institutions of learning. Children must know that they will be trained and controlled, or they will be punished and disciplined. Train up a child in the way he should go: and when he is old, he will not depart from it (Proverbs 22:6). The rod of correction may also have to be used (Proverbs 22:15).

When we refer to key ingredients within the community we are really getting to the type of value system that is prevalent within the community. When there is a lack of discipline, other things more easily get out of control very quickly, and lead to a multitude of problems for everyone in the community. Problems such as, a high crime rate, a high drop out rate, and a low literacy rate, which means that the cycle of desperation continues. There is the constant cry for Unity, but Unity needs a foundation to stand on and if our beliefs and standards are not moral and Just, the cry for Unity will just be an echo in the night that will not materialize. It is possible

99

to dream dreams that can't come true; but we can all study and work to make our communities a safer place to live and work.

The youth are impacted by the value system of the elder generation; they may have attempted to get into the young hip hop thing whatever that is, but they are really seeking a value system for their time. Their early training and upbringing should have taught them that we all need a solid value system and a continuity of purpose, if we are to remain committed and achieve our goals and objectives in life. We know not to judge any man, but you must be able to discern, and assess the character of those you choose to associate with, otherwise you may end up with negative influences, or those that are downright detrimental to you and your situation. Assess character before you grant access to you and all that you deem precious to you.

Unity will come naturally when we have the key ingredients within our community that Unity thrives upon. There must be discipline, training to obtain self-control and efficiency. We must have a continuity of purpose. Unity was and still is present on these isolated island communities where there is an obedience and respect of the elders, and I am convinced that they really do practice and live by the Golden Rule and the two Greatest Commandments (St. Matthew 22:35-40). We can all have Unity, but not without the ingredients of Unity.

Economic Development for a Better Community

Community Association – May be essential when there are peculiar problems or isolated community or an island community.

Economic Agenda – Should include the ownership and control of economic entities and educational institutions in the community.

Process for Change – Clearly define problems; Establish criteria; Use a pragmatic modus operandi to accomplish goals and objectives.

Establish Priorities – Consider the totality of circumstances!

Environmental Objectives – A good environment is essential for change; change environment, clean up environment you are in, associate with productive people. Clean up neighborhood and keep property clean, remove junk and abandoned vehicles. Continue personal development, continuing education, genealogy research (associations) etc.

Acquire Economic Skills – Essential for the economic development of the community.

Community Center with public facilities – This may be more essential for a community that is isolated or on an island.

Carolina – Still Home to Some Historically Black Colleges and Universities

Here in the Carolinas is where some of the historically Black colleges and universities are still thriving and in existence. Some of these colleges and universities educated many generations of Blacks, including many of my teachers that taught me during the 1950's. There is South Carolina State University in Orangeburg, Allen University, and Benedict College in Columbia, South Carolina. In North Carolina there still exist North Carolina A&T in Greensboro and Johnson C. Smith University in Charlotte.

These are the ones we mainly attended back in the days, and some of my high school classmates attended these schools in getting a higher education. Many of my grade school and high school teachers were from these historically Black colleges and universities. They were really dedicated teachers who saw to it that we were really prepared to move on into the bigger world after we graduated from high school in our little town way back then.

Our teachers were a major part of our community and some of them taught us in Sunday school and were very active in our churches. Some of them lived within walking distance of our house on our little dirt road, and we would all often walk to school taking shortcuts through vacant yards. They knew our parents very well and were often friends with our parents and would often drop by for visits. It was normal back then, but today if a teacher comes to visit a child's home it is probably because something went wrong at school or the student is having problems.

Some of the teachers would often come by our house to bring art projects for me to work on, especially around the holidays when they were having various plays and musicals at the churches. I enjoyed making those art projects for the various costumes and characters as it gave me a chance to practice my craft. The teachers were constantly involved with various community activities and were always anxious to help in any way they could. I was most impressed by their commitment and professionalism in the classroom. The dress was always appropriate and suits and ties were common and standard, even on our little small side of town. The Black colleges and universities had prepared them well, and they imparted their knowledge and keen insights to us, their very fortunate students.

The message they imparted to us back then was, to Study and Work, and you will be prepared to get ahead. They were there for us every step of the way and if we needed extra help in understanding something, they would take the necessary time to explain it to us until we got it. I will be eternally grateful that I had the opportunity to have such wonderful and dedicated teachers at a very young age helping mold my character. I can still remember my first grade teacher very vividly teaching us the alphabets, and her method was very effective and it didn't take most of us very long to learn the alphabets. The alphabets are something I always liked, and later on and even now I often recite them forwards and backwards.

The historically Black colleges and universities in this area have a long history of turning out dedicated and committed teachers. They have a long and very rich history, and have always been in the forefront for change for generations.

The students have always been very active and not afraid to stand up for change and for what's right. They have stood up for what's right even when they didn't get any credit for it by the wider media or those on the outside. The students at South Carolina State University in Orangeburg organized a boycott of the town's businesses in 1956, long before it was popular to do such things. Some of the students sacrificed and stood up for what they believed in, and that helped paved the way for a better day that we have now. Some of them were expelled from school, but that did not prevent them from making their impact lasting and profound. They stood up and boycotted, and this was over a decade before the 1968 Orangeburg massacre, which is still not fully documented to this day.

History will pass some events by unless we who have personal knowledge of such events take the time to document and record our past experiences and recollections. We who were there or have the facts, and have personal knowledge of the events and occurrences must document and record them so that they will not be overlooked in history.

The students who took part in those boycotts and protests really stood up before Rosa Parks sat down on the bus. But even though they didn't get the publicity or credit that others after them may have gotten, we are just as grateful to them for standing up for what they believed in and making it better for us all today.

We all had roles to play even way back then. I never got the opportunity to attend one of those historically Black colleges and universities. But I surely benefited from them being here imparting knowledge to our precious dedicated teachers, who were really prepared to teach us as we attended our little rural schools here all up and down the Carolina Lowcountry and beyond. We could not all afford to attend college right after high school in those days as there was little financial aid available.

Many of our ministers were from those historically Black colleges and universities, and the teaching and guidance they gave us in our little Bible belt communities really laid a strong foundation for us to practice our faith and beliefs. Their contributions way back then in our small rural communities are still felt today and has even impacted the present generation. That is quite evident by the large number of people that keep coming back to the old reunions and retreats each and every year.

I often pause and reflect on those old days back then. I remember studying at home when all that we had for light were the old kerosene lamps in the days before electricity came to our little neighborhood on those dirt roads. That did not stop me from learning or attending Bible classes during our summer Bible school that we had at our church, and Bible school was something that I always looked forward to. In that house today that was built in 1946, are two of those old kerosene lamps sitting on the dresser in the main bedroom, as a constant reminder to me of what it used to be like, and how far we have come and accomplished through study and hard work.

Even though I didn't go to college in the Carolinas, as I migrated to California to attend college virtually free. The Carolina Lowcountry experience had laid a deep foundation for my success in the California colleges and universities. I remembered the dedication and commitment of my teachers from those small historically Black colleges and universities, and carried it over with me as I attended college so many miles away from home. I took a Trailways Bus from South Carolina all the way to California in 1961, as it was the only transportation we could afford back then. I knew then that the race was not given to the swift, nor the battle to the strong, but that time and chance happeneth to them all (Ecclesiastes 9:11).

The sight of the San Francisco night skyline as the old Trailways Bus was going across the San Francisco-Oakland Bay Bridge on its way into San Francisco is a night sight that I will never forget. I had never seen so many big city lights in my life as I was coming from such a small rural town way down on the Carolina Lowcountry. I knew then that I would really study and work hard and be successful because I did not want to take another cross country trip on a Trailways Bus ever again.

I quickly adjusted to the big city life while maintaining my Bible belt value system. I also attended for a time the Academy of Art College when its main building was on Sutter Street in downtown San Francisco. In fact I was attending an art class when we got word that Dr. Martin Luther King Jr. was assassinated. The whole school seemed to get extra quiet as the word got passed around. I eventually obtained a job working as a production artist in the city.

I would often pause and reflect while sitting at my drawing board on Howard Street as I was looking up New Montgomery Street in San Francisco. I knew then that I would have to document and record the events that I was experiencing. I began to put on paper many of the experiences we had here in the Carolina Lowcountry, especially my experiences on Sandy Island. I wrote a term paper on life on Sandy Island for one of my classes at San Francisco State University, and I got an A on it. In one of my many moves in and out of apartments, the paper was lost, but that did not stop me and I continued to rewrite the paper. These were the days before computers and easy back ups on discs, etc. So even if delays come it is important for us to continue on after we get up as many times as we fall, for we must accomplish our goals and objectives.

So even as communities are changing, changed or gone we have a very strong foundation and a never ending commitment to continue on and succeed. We know that we have what it takes to make a better day in the midst of these rapidly changing times. For we have come from and experienced what it's like to come from so far below the water line.

As we look up and down the Carolina Lowcountry at our past, present and future; we can be assured that the institutions that we hold dearly, our churches and schools have survived, and so have we to move on to an even greater day. The historically Black colleges and universities are still imparting knowledge, uplifting and empowering even more generations as the decades have passed. These colleges and universities are truly a beautiful part of our culture and heritage, and a continuing beacon in the night and long day as we keep marching on to even better achievements.

This applies equally true to the many other historically Black colleges and universities beyond the borders of the Carolinas. Many of our teachers here in the Carolina Lowcountry were from those colleges and universities beyond our borders. We all knew of the history of many

107

of those colleges and universities, such as Fisk University and the history of the Fisk Jubilee Singers. We knew of Meharry Medical College, and the complex of colleges in Atlanta, especially Morehouse College and the King's family legacy. We knew the history of Tuskegee Institute and the Tuskegee Airmen, Frederick Douglas and Booker T. Washington. We also knew of the "Tuskegee Experiment" on Black men, which showed man's inhumanity toward man. We knew the history of Southern University and Grambling University and Tennessee A&I, etc. They all were making a great contribution to us no matter where we lived, because the students they prepared made it better and easier for us to succeed.

These historically Black colleges and universities were critical to our progress, as they prepared the generations that returned to us in our little small rural communities to teach us so that we would be prepared to face life's challenges ahead. Their legacy is a beautiful part of our culture and heritage. Many of these historically Black colleges and universities are still operating and carrying on in the tradition of making life better for all in these rapidly changing times.

The Gullah lifestyle, history and culture as passed down from the Sea Island slaves, is still alive and flourishing here along the Carolina Lowcountry.

The historically Black colleges and universities
have prepared many generations for the
challenges of life

The achievements of the Tuskegee Airmen is
something that everyone should be proud of,
and history will always remember them

Many great professional athletes came from these historically Black colleges and universities

Jerry Rice - MVP
Super Bowl XXIII

These athletes have gone on to have great careers and many are in the Hall of Fame

We are indebted to all of our great trailblazers, no matter where they went to school, for they showed the way by their great examples

Gullah History and Culture is Alive and Flourishing Along The Carolina Lowcountry

The Gullah history and culture is still alive and flourishing here along the Carolina Lowcountry and beyond. The countryside and surrounding areas have changed somewhat over time, and different generations primarily stroll here now. All up and down the area you can see the concerted efforts of the people to preserve their culture. Some of the older generation have returned and set up various little shops with artifacts and other cultural items for sale.

Some of the older generation that is returning are craftsmen and artists who have returned to continue practicing their arts, and to pass down their skills to yet another generation. Some of them received some unique skills from their ancestors and continued practicing their crafts even though far away from home. Many of the skills were passed down from generation to generation, such as, the making of sweet grass baskets, etc. which are still made and sold in the area today.

The culture passed down from Sea Island slaves on isolated barrier islands still continue to have a very profound effect on their descendants today. Some of their direct descendants still reside on a few of those old isolated islands carrying on in the tradition of their ancestors. They are keenly aware that they are actually living in a perpetual museum. Their homes are now equipped with all the modern conveniences of life, but they remain in physical isolation, especially on isolated islands such as, Sandy Island. The people that reside on these isolated islands today are there because they chose to be there, and will not have it any other way.

114

They are really connected with the traditions of their ancestors. The Gullah people, even today seem to genuinely enjoy living away from the mainland, and it's as if they don't recognize or acknowledge the physical isolation. I often stand at the Sandy Island Landing, or at the bank of the Waccamaw River and watch the people in their small motor boats make their way across the river to their homes on the isolated island. They'll take the same old sandy unimproved roads on their isolated island to their homes tucked away back in time.

Many tourists now come to our area of the Carolina Lowcountry, especially the Myrtle Beach Grand Strand, now that major development is here. Many of the tourists remain interested in the history and culture of the people in the area, and there are now many tours offered to see almost anything you want to see that is historic. There are tours of the historic sections of historic towns and cities, old plantations, museums, etc. The Penn Center is a major attraction for tourists and is dedicated to preserving the Gullah history and culture.

One can get a sense of what life must have been like centuries ago on the old rice plantations, some with old cabins restored, etc. I just look at some of the old cabins and villages and wonder what it must have been like living here over a century ago. I have copies of photographs that were taken of my grandmother during the early 1940's as she stood in the field working with two of her grandkids nearby. I cherish looking at many of the other old photographs that we have of some of the old days. I look and see the field where my grandmother was standing was later a peanut field, and I remember that I helped harvest the peanuts. I remember helping to put the green peanuts just taken out of the ground in a big stack against a pole so that the peanuts could dry.

There are still some serene days here in the county now. It's wonderful to see life here today in some of our communities that have survived so much over the decades and centuries. Life on the isolated island is a little different now with instant communications, etc. I now go over to the island and beyond taking pictures with my camcorder in order to further capture the natural and pristine scenes and settings that I thought would have been lost decades ago. Some of the scenes that I have captured today are the same scenes that I saw on that old isolated island over a half century ago. The only thing that has changed now are the people in the pictures are of the current generation, as there's just a very few of the old timer's left.

I see the many alumni's returning with their cameras and recording their history, and some have resettled back home to further carry on in the traditions of their ancestors. Another thing that has not changed much are the rivers, the mighty black water Waccamaw River is just as ferocious as ever as it goes a-roaring downriver. The Great Pee Dee River still rolls along the western border of Sandy Island, and just across that river is Plantersville, the hometown of my mother. The mighty Waccamaw River still connects up with the Great Pee Dee River just south of Sandy Island, as the two rivers meet up at Winyah bay at Georgetown as they go rolling along on their way to the Atlantic Ocean.

The rivers, inlets, bays, etc. in the Carolina Lowcountry all have a rich history, and have contributed much to the quality of life all along it's banks and beyond. The rivers and waters have always supported an abundance of life in and out of the waters. If such rivers and waters were not in such close proximity a lot of the prior generations may not have survived, as the rivers provided food, etc.

116

I enjoyed eating fresh water fish, and always looked forward to those big cook outs and fish fries. I know that I have eaten many a meals from the rivers and inlets, waters, etc. along the Carolina Lowcountry.

As I journey back to the rivers and surrounding fishing areas I still see many a people fishing. Some are fishing today because they enjoy fishing, and are not fishing because they are desperate for food. You can still see a few of the old timers fishing near the bank of the river right alongside the youngsters. It seems that each generation has found something unique about the river. Many return to their favorite spots along the riverbank after being away for decades. They don't fish there all the time, and sometimes you will see them there with their children and grandchildren teaching them some of the history of the area.

I constantly marvel at the many historic scenes that I have seen right there before my eyes as I stood there looking at three generations reflecting on their history and culture. Many of the people now have much more than their ancestors had, or so it appears that way. In my young days visiting on the isolated island, the live stocks could just roam all over the island in unchecked freedom. Today live stocks cannot roam on the island portion that is not your land, and neither can you. Some of the younger generation acquired jeeps, etc. but they cannot roam all over the island as we did growing up.

Each generation is somewhat different, perhaps because each generation lives in a different part of history. It seems like the more the current generation acquires in certain material things, the more they don't have in some of the things that really matter. When I was a kid my primary mode of transportation was my bicycle.

117

I even went shopping downtown with my bicycle and bringing back the groceries in my basket on my bicycle was a special joy to me. That was a little something that I could do to help my parents. I didn't miss having a car because cars were something I really didn't think about much. We concentrated on making the most out of the situation that we were confronted with, and to enjoy life with what we had at the moment. Tomorrow is not promised to us, but we can have a better tomorrow if we become prepared today with what we have and just do it.

We should document and record that which we have experienced and know is for real; changes are still a-coming and will pass over your precious history. You were there, and you are here now, so you must document and record it, or it may not get done when you leave your sojourn here among us. Let us stop, pause, and reflect, and move on to an even better day.

May God bless and keep us all in our pursuits to document and record that which we have experienced here, for it is a beautiful and precious part of our culture and heritage. Our sojourn here was for a very special purpose, and we should be able to say, well done, Amen.

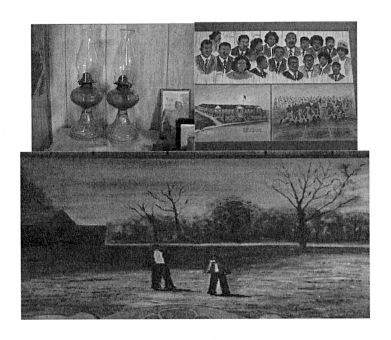

Many things have changed since those early
years so many decades ago, but the desire and
commitment of the people is still strong

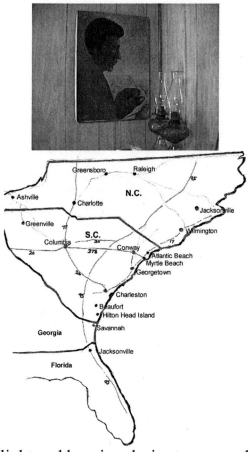

The light and burning desire to succeed still
exist all up and down the Carolina Lowcountry
and beyond

It carried me through some difficult days many decades ago a long, long way from home

There were also many good days a long way from home

Some of the old scenes have gone on into
posterity now, but the river keeps rolling on

As we walk down the uncertain paths today and approach the critical crossroads in life, our faith must be strong and on solid ground

THE SOUL OF TOM PYATT
SAN FRANCISCO, CALIF.

LOOKING UP NEW MONTGOMERY ST.
SITTING AT MY DRAWING BOARD AT
639 HOWARD ST . . . . 6\12\75

And as I sit at my drawing board I'll continue to document and record the magnificent history and culture of the Gullah people here in the Carolina Lowcountry and beyond

That View

That is the view of the life and times of the people and their communities along the Carolina Lowcountry, as seen from my perspective and vantage point.

A look back at the history of the area, the traditions, customs, habits, and folkways of the people. To document and record the history of a unique people and their culture.

The Lowcountry is full of a very deep history of all its' people, and is the home of many cultures. Even in the midst of the many changes and development, it is still apparent that the spirit of the people is to continue working to make it better for all.

Art Director – T.J. Pyatt
www.tjpyatt.com

125

Index